Praise for

Remembrances

"A personal friend for some 40 years now, Charlie Norman is a fellow weaver of words. His skill at telling a story with vivid imagery and engaging detail makes for unforgettable reading that will warm your heart and encourage your soul."

— Steve Chapman, singer/songwriter and bestselling author of *The Tales Hunters Tell* and *A Look at Life from the Riverbank: Stories About Fishing and the Meaning of Life*

"My long-time and good friend Charlie Norman is not a doctor, but with his writing he provides a wonderful, daily dose of encouragement, inspiration, grins, chuckles, and laughs. Enjoy!"

— "Randy Mac" McLelland, pastor, author, humorist, and master storyteller

Remembrances

CHARLES H. NORMAN III

Remembrances
Charles H. Norman III

Published May 2021
Heirloom Editions
Imprint of Jan-Carol Publishing, Inc.
All rights reserved
Copyright © 2021 Charles H. Norman III

This book may not be reproduced in whole or part,
in any manner whatsoever, without written permission,
with the exception of brief quotations within book reviews or articles.

ISBN: 978-1-954978-04-1
Library of Congress Control Number: 20219369995

You may contact the publisher:
Jan-Carol Publishing, Inc.
PO Box 701
Johnson City, TN 37605
publisher@jancarolpublishing.com
www.jancarolpublishing.com

PREFACE

A few years ago, the opportunity for me to become a monthly "Guest Community Columnist" for *The Glen Rose Reporter*, my little Texas hometown's weekly newspaper, presented itself to me. I thought, *Well, I am a storyteller of sorts, and I have done a little nonprofessional writing in my seventy years, so maybe I'll write something and submit it for consideration.* I did, and they liked it. Three years later, I'm still submitting.

Through the years, several friends have told me how much they've enjoyed my articles, and they suggested that I consider compiling these anecdotal stories and turning them into a book, if only for posterity or close friends. *Remembrances* is a product of that idea. I hope that maybe, in a small way, these true-to-life stories will encourage, entertain, or challenge you along your way. These *remembrances* are of a blessed life, and I'm honored to share them with you. Thanks for reading.

Charles H. Norman III

TABLE OF CONTENTS

1. Being Second Ain't So Bad...1
2. Reconciliation 150 Years Ago Is Still Felt Today..................................4
3. "Hoppy Dogs," Anyone?...7
4. Friends Closer Than a Brother?..10
5. Everybody's Favorite Is Still Remembered..13
6. My Banner Year with the Little Ladies..16
7. Spinning Through Town with the Oldies but Goodies......................19
8. When Fathers Become Heroes..22
9. Little Decisions Make Big Impact..25
10. Fitting Name for a Fellow I Know..28
11. Expect the Unexpected at School Reunions......................................31
12. Trading Football Cleats for Dancing Shoes......................................34
13. Deliverance Day Celebrated Each Year..37
14. More Than I Bargained For..42
15. The Ring That Was Never Lost..46

16. Let the Healing Begin..50

17. No More Problems with "Acoustics"...................................54

18. "Puki" — Big Dog in a Little Package...............................57

19. Quest for a Trophy..60

20. A Mother's Love Is Never Forgotten..................................63

21. Grandkids See a Different Side of Daddy O......................66

22. Proud to Be #3...69

23. A Present-Day Fisher of Men...72

24. Return Dog to Sender..75

25. September 11, 2001–Why Not Me?..................................78

26. Rooting for the Underdog..81

27. You've Got a Friend in Me...84

28. Bird Rehab Brings Rich Rewards.......................................88

29. Respect for a Man of Honor..91

30. Be Careful What You Wish For...95

31. WWII Vet Is Still the Teacher..99

32. Happy He Will Be...103

About the Author...107

1
BEING SECOND AIN'T SO BAD

When I was growing up in the dusty West Texas plains of Odessa in the late 1950s and early 1960s, it seemed like everything of importance in my world revolved around school and sports. We didn't have lakes nearby to fish in, trails to hike, or many trees to climb (ever heard of Notrees, TX? It's an actual place out there). But we did have baseball. Think *The Sandlot*. So, there I was, a scrawny little sixth grader, trying out for the Austin Elementary baseball team. Man, I was ready for the big league. Blue and gold were our colors, and I always liked those colors. Our uniforms consisted of overly worn, faded, goldish-colored T-shirts with dark-blue numerals, but I didn't care. I was on a team representing Austin, *my* school.

Anyway, Coach Harrison assigned me to play second base. And I did pretty good, too. You see, my dad had taken me down to the Athletic Supply store on Grant Avenue so I could pick out a baseball glove of my very own. It didn't take me long to pick out a Nocona-made, black leather glove. Boy, did I feel proud! Dad had then worked with me some in our front yard, teaching me how to catch grounders and popups until I got the hang of it, and then I'd started practicing on my own and with friends. I played second base all year long. That was my spot. At the end of the season, for making the fewest errors, Coach Harrison awarded me with a baseball that had been signed by him and my teammates. From then on, whenever I played baseball or softball (whether I was playing during school intramurals and or outside of school), I just seemed to naturally gravitate toward second base. I was comfortable there and felt at home. That was my position.

Fast-forward some thirty-five years later. My dad mentioned on the phone that he'd run into ol' Coach Harrison, who had been working part-time at Melvin's Clothiers since retiring from teaching and coaching.

"Really, Dad? It'd sure be great to see him the next time I'm out that way. I'd like to tell him about the good memories I have of playing for him!" I said.

So, it was around 1995 or so when I drove over to see my old coach at his modest home. It felt strange seeing him after that long. I was then a middle-aged adult, and the last time I had seen him, I was just a kid. It was just different. I told Coach Tommy Harrison about the fond memories I had of him and of the way he treated us kids. I thanked him for being my coach. And then I asked him a question I'd thought about all of those years I hadn't seen him: "Coach, I was just wondering, why did you put me at second base? I mean, that's the position I've played ever since. Was it because I was maybe 'shifty around the base pads,' because you knew I could handle those 'hot' grounders coming my way, or possibly because you thought I could work that double play ball?"

Silence. Looking a little perplexed at first, he then responded, "Well, Charlie, I don't know. Can't remember. But I usually put the kid with the weakest arm on second."

What?!! Excuse me!! There I was, thinking I might receive a little "ego boost," and it wasn't happening. After I recovered a bit from that revelation (still not completely over it! NOT!), I glanced up at this elderly man from my past. I thanked him again for being part of my life, and I meant it. Knowing I'd probably never see or speak to him again, I teared up a little as I drove off. I was so glad I went. I like to think I helped him have a better day that day, and I wanted him to know he was appreciated and hadn't been forgotten, even after all of those years, which was actually the real purpose of my visit in the first place. I would still choose to play second base if given the opportunity.

My original Nocona-made glove from 1961.

2
RECONCILIATION 150 YEARS AGO IS STILL FELT TODAY

A few years ago, I ventured to East Tennessee during a quest to find out more about my ancestors from my dad's side of the family. I hadn't gotten into ancestry.com or similar websites at that time. I knew some things about the family because I'd saved some of my great aunt's old letters and notes, along with a century-old book about the history of Sullivan County, TN. Aside from that information, all I knew was that my paternal grandfather, Charles Henry Norman, Sr., was born in Bristol, TN, in 1891. So, after a two-hour flight to Knoxville, I arrived in Tennessee and drove another 90 miles northeast to Sullivan County and to the small town of Blountville, where I found the historical records/genealogy building for the county (about nine miles south of Bristol). Upon entering the building, I was warmly greeted by the curator and director of the Sullivan County Department of Archives. I told her what I was looking for and asked if she could help me get started with resources in the library. Well, she sure would. But first, she made it very clear that there were certain stipulations and protocols I had to agree to follow before being allowed access to the books, records, and archives. No laptops or photography permitted, only one resource at a time, and items had to be handled in a very specific manner.

All of this was okay with me. I just wanted to know more about Grandfather Norman and my ancestors. The curator said she'd do a little research herself and would let me know if she came across anything. Well, after about ten minutes, she came over to me, plopped down a couple of printed-out sheets, and very satisfactorily announced, "Well, Mr. Norman, we're family. You're my sixth cousin." Whoa! "And your great-great-grandfather, Thomas Jefferson Norman, is buried about ten miles from here, in the cemetery next to what is now Arcadia United Methodist Church."

How fun was this! I had to go there! But before I went, I was able to learn more about this distant relative. Come to find out, in the 1890 US Census, he had been registered as one of thirty surviving Civil War veterans still living in Sullivan County. He'd fought on the side of the Union. History buffs would know that although Tennessee was officially a Confederate state, there were certain regions, especially in the northeastern portion of the state, that were particularly divided, and many times friends, neighbors, and family members were on opposite sides of the war. I can't imagine what heartache and agony these folks must have gone through. Further research revealed that after the war, my great-great-grandfather, Thomas Jefferson Norman, named his second son (the first born after the Civil War), Joseph Henry Norman (b. 1869), after local hero, educator, philanthropist, and seminary founder Joseph Henry Ketron. Both my great-great-grandfather Thomas and his schoolmate Joseph were

Charles III and Charles IV

born in 1837. They had attended the same church and must have been good friends all their lives.

Later that day, I went to Kingsport, TN, and reverently walked in and around the little country church's cemetery, where numerous Norman kinsfolk were buried. Planted next to Thomas Jefferson Norman's gravestone (1837-1923) was a small US flag. I have to say that it felt a little surreal standing right there, knowing that less than a hundred years ago, a contingent of family members who had the same last name as me must have gathered there.

As I ventured a few feet away, I came across the gravestone of Joseph Henry Ketron (1837-1908). Next to it, there was a little Confederate flag *and* a United States flag. It took me a while before I realized the significance. It dawned on me that though they were strong adversaries for four tumultuous years (1861-1865), my great-great-grandfather still named his son after his neighbor, peer, and lifelong friend. What a special relationship they must have had! Forgiveness, reconciliation, and admiration had overcome pride, bitterness, and division. After putting aside the past deep, deep conflict and laying down their arms, these two men reached out to each other because they had genuine respect and love for each other as human beings and as fellow citizens of this great country. Sounds like something we Americans might need to do more often, wouldn't you say? I think so.

P.S. My middle name is Henry, so in essence, I proudly bear a portion of these two men's names, and I feel honored every time I write my full name, Charles Henry Norman III.

3
"HOPPY DOGS," ANYONE?

A few years back, when the family attended church in Glen Rose, I would periodically drive the church van to pick up a few folks who needed a ride. It was a privilege to do this. There was one stop in particular that I always looked forward to. It was just a couple of blocks away from the square, and it was affectionately known as the "Group House." There'd usually be two or three young to middle-aged men waiting by the curb. All of these guys had special needs and/or physical limitations.

There was one fellow in the group whom I was especially drawn to. His name was Doug. Doug had Down's syndrome. Doug was sweet, gentle, kind, friendly, PUNCTUAL, and a little naïve in his own way, which are qualities we could all probably use more of. Everybody loved Doug. Sometimes he'd sit next to us in church, and he listened and sang along pretty well, too. Every so often, I'd glance over at Doug and observe him and the fascination he had with his shiny new wristwatch. Simple things.

Sometimes my family would ride with me when I went to pick people up. By doing this, they got to know Doug, too. Somehow, over time, we started conversing with Doug by asking him easy yes-or-no questions along the way. We would ask something like, "Having a good day, Doug?"

or "Like going to church?" or "Enjoy your breakfast this morning, Doug?" He'd almost always emphatically answer with a "Yea-ah!" That was Doug.

As we got to know him better, we'd ask other things, such as, "What'd you have for breakfast, Doug?"

"Pancakes!" was his answer.

"You like pancakes, Doug?" we'd ask.

"Yea-ah!" he said.

"What's your favorite food, Doug?"

"Hoppy dogs!" (We just had to chuckle.)

"You like Hoppy dogs, Doug?"

"Yea-ah!"

"Well, we like Hoppy Dogs too!"

So sweet, so innocent, so Doug.

Later, after we were all more comfortable with each other, I decided I'd ask him some crazy, made-up questions, such as, "Doug, you ever had deep-fried camel-hump patties for lunch?" or "Would you like to try some sautéed salamander slivers?" He'd always be quick to answer loudly, "Na-aw!" And we'd all laugh together.

I sensed that he enjoyed the interaction. It certainly made the ride to church all the more enjoyable.

One particular Sunday, it was just me and Doug. As I was about to assist him into the van, he indicated that he wanted me to help him tie his tie. Okay. When I finished, he indicated that he wasn't quite satisfied with the way it looked. I had *not* put the tail end of the tie through the "keeper's loop" (that extra piece of fabric sewn on the backside of the tie; it keeps the tail out of view). The thing is, I was a college graduate and had been tying ties for around forty years, but I had never thought about what that was for (I'd always just used a tie clasp)! Doug taught me something that day, and it was about more than just tying a tie. Simple folks sometimes have simple ways, and sometimes they just like things done a certain way. And that's quite okay. You know what else? They just might know things we "highly educated" people don't know.

Doug passed away several years ago and is in heaven now. I've never forgotten him or what I learned from that meek, simple soul. I have a feeling that when I get to heaven one day, I'll be seeing ol' Doug again, and he just might teach me another thing or two. It'd be an honor.

4

FRIENDS CLOSER THAN A BROTHER

Fourteen years ago, on Valentine's Day weekend, I found myself at St. Joseph's Hospital in Bryan, TX, praying for the life and recovery of my son Charles IV. A college freshman at Texas A&M, Charles had told his mom — my wife, Carolyn — on the phone the night before that he was not feeling "quite right." Upon her urging, he agreed to go to the school infirmary the next day. So, early that Friday morning, Charles started walking to the clinic, only to become quite disoriented and delusional. He somehow managed to stagger his way through the infirmary's doors. After a quick evaluation, the medical staff realized this was beyond their scope of treatment and called for an ambulance that would transport him to St. Joseph, a few miles away. The nurse called Carolyn, who was in Glen Rose, to inform her of the situation, and within two and a half hours, Carolyn was there at his bedside in the ER.

I was in Denver when I received Carolyn's call, and I was able to catch a couple of flights and get there by late afternoon. I'll never forget the gut-wrenching, sick feeling I had when Charles first spotted me. He sat up, his arms flailing. There was a distant, hollow look in his eyes, and he could only speak gibberish.

Initial tests were inconclusive, but the doctor said he was going to treat him for viral encephalitis. He put him on intravenous fluids and ordered further tests, including an MRI of the brain and an EEG, which were both scheduled for early Saturday morning. Charles lay there, unresponsive, as Carolyn slept on the couch in his hospital room that night. I slept out in the car, wondering if it was all just a bad dream.

Late that Saturday morning, the doctor came in and said, "Though the tests are not definitive, there is slight swelling of the brain, and we're going to continue treating him for viral encephalitis. There is no cure, but we treat the symptoms as best as we can until the virus has run its course. Intravenous fluids, rest, continual monitoring, time, and prayer are what we've got." I asked the doctor what the prognosis was for such a condition. He said that some people heal completely and have no aftereffects, some only regain partial faculties, and some never recover.

Carolyn was crying, and she said, "All I want is to have my son back and for him to be normal again." Oh Lord, me, too.

We asked for prayers from our close friends whom we knew to be believers. There was no noticeable change throughout the day. Carolyn got a call from the infirmary nurse at A&M. She was calling to check on Charles, and Carolyn decided to accept her invitation to spend the night at her house and get away for a few hours. We thought that was a good idea. I just stayed in my son's room alone, praying and sleeping the night away.

Around 10:00 p.m., I heard a knock on the door, and it Caleb, Sarah, and Carrie, who were three of Charles's close college friends. They asked if they could come in to pray for Charles. "Oh yes, please," I said. I expected them to circle around his bed and have between five and ten minutes of prayer for my son. But they had other ideas. Carrie knelt down on that hard linoleum floor, right at the foot of the bed, and Caleb and Sarah got on their knees on each side, placing their ministering hands on Charles. For almost an hour, they beseeched the Lord on Charles's behalf! I was in grateful awe of these three young college friends who were giving up their time on a Saturday night so they could come pray for my son. Though Charles probably did not hear any of those prayers, I certainly did. Even more importantly, I believe The Great Physician heard. I hugged these three young people in humble gratitude, and Proverbs 18:24 came to mind: "There is a friend/s that sticks closer than a brother." I had just witnessed that, and it was true love in action.

I lay on the couch that night, listening to the constant drip of nourishing fluids that were entering my son's body. With each drop, I whispered the sweetest name I know: "Jesus...Jesus...Jesus." I did this until I dozed off, and then the Sunday morning light woke me the next morning.

The nurse came in, did her morning check of the monitors, and said, "Hmm, things seem to be a little better. The doctor should be in shortly." What encouraging news!

In the meantime, Charles was beginning to stir a bit, as well. The doctor entered, did his evaluation, and said there was definite improvement! Carolyn and I embraced each other, crying tears of hope and thankfulness. We were thankful for faithful friends who had prayed for healing; doctors and specialists who had used their intelligence, education, and training to help others; and the Good Lord, who heard our prayers and honored our great desire.

Charles improved so quickly throughout the day that that when the doctor came around to evaluate him for the second time later that afternoon, we heard the words we'd longed for only forty-eight hours before: "I think Charles will be well enough to get out of here in the morning, and he can go to class by afternoon."

Charles, with a sly grin on his face, then spoke up, saying, "Do I have to?" We then knew he was normal again. It was the best Valentine's gift ever!

5
EVERYBODY'S FAVORITE IS STILL REMEMBERED

In a couple of months, I'll be headed off to Odessa with my wife, Carolyn, for my fifty-year high school reunion. She has faithfully tagged along to a number of my past reunions and has told me more than once that my former classmates have welcomed her with open arms and made her feel right at home. Back in 1983 (for my fifteen-year reunion, her first with me), Carolyn and I had been married only a few years, and I was very much looking forward to introducing my Tennessee gal to the friends I had grown up with in Texas. One fellow student I especially wanted her to meet was everybody's favorite, Becky Rhodes.

Becky and I had attended Austin Elementary together for years, but it was in the eighth grade that I took a particular liking to this special gal. She was sharp, funny, sweet, witty, kind, and just plain fun, and she treated everyone like a friend. I liked that. While Becky was not really the "classic beauty," at least as some might understand the word, she possessed an inward beauty that served as her allure and attractiveness. I was too immature to comprehend all of that. All I knew was that I liked Becky. Although she stood at least six inches taller than me, I decided that at the high school football game on Friday night, I was going to ask Becky to "go steady and be my girlfriend." Well, the big day came, and though I tried, I just couldn't muster up the courage to ask her. So, my best bud, Richard, got frustrated and blurted out to me, "You want me to ask her for you?"

I hemmed and hawed around and finally said, "Okay, would you?"

Next thing I knew, he was scurrying over a couple of bleachers, doing the deed, and hollering back at me, "She said yes!"

I was very pleased (and relieved) and knew it was just a matter of time until I'd be holding her hand. When I got home, I couldn't wait to tell my daddy that the most popular gal in school was my girlfriend. His response: "Don't you think you're a little too young to have a steady girlfriend?" What a downer! His comment to me severely dampened my enthusiasm about my new, next-level friendship with Becky. Yet I was still determined. By golly, I was going to hold her hand at the next Friday night game, which was on November 22, 1963. The day our country lost a president. Though the game went on, it was if the players, the fans, and the students were all in a stupor. Becky did not show, and my thought-out plan was in disarray.

My courage to reach out waned with each passing day. It just wasn't the same. After a couple of weeks or so, Becky and I talked and decided it would be best if we went back to being "just good friends" again. Whew! Funny how within a three-week span, I was *relieved* twice, and for the opposite reasons! Go figure.

For the next five years of school, Becky's popularity only

grew. She was the 1967 OHS homecoming queen, senior class favorite, Miss Odessa High School, and on and on. What was there not to like about Becky? Shoot, at a previous reunion, I even heard one popular cheerleader tell her daughter that though she had been a candidate herself, she, too, had voted for Becky for homecoming queen. That says something to me about both ladies.

All this being said, when my mom called me back in early 1983 (before the fifteen-year reunion) and told me that Becky, only thirty-three, had passed away after fighting an aggressive form of cancer, I was absolutely stunned. It felt like I had been punched in the stomach. How could this be? I hadn't even known she was ill. Of all people, she was one who deserved a long and productive life. She brought smiles, laughter, and a sense of worth to everyone she knew.

As I think back on this now, I wonder how it is that I've lived over twice as long as she lived. I reflect on others in my class who have also passed on. Some passed decades ago, and some passed only recently. I pause and ponder. Then I think of how the Good Book encourages us all to count each day as a gift. We are supposed to use wisely the time given to us by our Creator. Remember to be thankful. And thankful, I am. I am also sure that if Becky and Carolyn had ever met, they would have bonded immediately and would have become fast friends from the get-go. Knowing my Carolyn, she would have voted for Becky, too.

6
MY BANNER YEAR WITH THE LITTLE LADIES

Always liked the girls, I did. I can't remember a time when I didn't like having the gals around. In the first grade, my teacher caught me chasing Sharon around the classroom. She had stolen my Easter basket after I tried to "kiss" her on the elbow (I don't know, either). We each got a paddling in the bookroom because of our misbehavior. Didn't mind a bit. It hurt so good. Besides, it was a "bonding experience."

But the fifth grade...now, that was my "Banner Year" with the little ladies. For a few weeks back in the sixties, I had five girlfriends at one time! Hey, hey! I guess I was too naïve and inexperienced to know that that was probably not the proper or cool thing to do. Carolyn reminds me *not* to get the "big head" over something that happened around fifty-five years ago. Whatever. Let's see, there was sweet little Linda, fresh-faced Nancy, and Helen with the big dimples. Lou Ann was different, though; she claimed *me* as her boyfriend. Though I liked her somewhat, she was twice my size, and I was actually a little afraid *not* to be her boyfriend.

But my favorite of all was Katrina. She had long black hair and a beautiful smile, and she possessed a certain coyness that made her all the more alluring. I was smitten. Shoot, I just liked her name. I had never known a "Katrina" before. One fine day, I asked her to come watch me play basketball when our school team, the Austin Elementary Blue and Gold, was facing off against the Black and Gold team from Cameron Elementary. She came, and as fate would have it, I scored the first four points of our 10-4 blowout victory over our opponents. Man, I felt like a hero. I even got to take a short five-minute walk with Katrina outside and around the school after the game ended, and I...held her hand! Heady stuff for a ten-year-old.

Christmas break came, and my parents got me a miniature black French poodle as my main present. Oh, how I loved that puppy. She was sweet, smart, and obedient, and she always wanted to please. Best dog ever! So I named her Katrina. When classes resumed after the holiday, I couldn't wait to tell Katrina the news. "Katrina, I like you so much that I named my dog after you." Uh oh...I didn't get quite the reaction I had expected. For some reason, things were never the same between us. I didn't understand. My dad tried consoling me by explaining that that was just the way life was. He said that we fellas can't understand women. Katrina dropped me for an upperclassman, a sixth grader named Arnold, whom she rode the bus with every day. I felt jealous pangs for the first time, and I've never cared much for the name "Arnold" since. Because of all of that, I actually started calling my dog "Trina" for short, as it hurt too much to say the whole name. Trina was my constant and loyal companion for fifteen wonderful years.

But it wasn't long until Crockett Jr. High beckoned me in, and a whole new bevy of little lasses entered my world. Let's see, there was the cheerleader Jan, class favorite Vickie (so pretty that all of us boys were intimidated), and CJHS band sweetheart and majorette Brenda. Can't forget Marsha, either. She ended up being my first date ever when I took her to the freshman prom (my dad served as chauffeur).

But the moral of the story is this: DO NOT name your dog after your girlfriend (or at least don't tell her you did).

By the way, things ended up quite nicely for me. I married a pretty gal with big ol' dimples, and after thirty-five years we still like each other.

I'm in the first row, second boy from left; Katrina's right behind me.

7

SPINNING THROUGH TOWN WITH THE OLDIES BUT GOODIES

A couple of years ago, I finally acquired my "dream car." For over fifty years, I'd been wanting to own a red 1965 Ford Mustang. I wanted it to be sporty and classy, though not too big or expensive. With the blessing of Carolyn, and her assistance, my dream became reality. She found it at an estate sale auction up near Crowley and put a bid on it, and a few hours later we got the call that she was the top bidder on "Little Red." For the next year or so, I took great pride in getting it all spruced up — new red upholstery/carpet, new steering wheel, new whitewall tires, and new air conditioning. How satisfying it was to see it all come together!

Throughout the process, though, I was contemplating how I could share my good fortune with others without seeming pretentious. Carolyn had an idea: "Why not take certain people out for a spin. You know, those who can't get around much anymore. And then treat 'em to lunch." Yes, I could do that! So, for over a year now, that has been my great privilege. I made arrangements with the director at one of the local nursing homes, and she selects individuals who are able and might like to go out for lunch. I take them to the places of their choosing and then drive around Glen Rose for a few minutes.

I will say that most of the time, it's a little bit of a challenge to converse with my riders, as their answers to my tender inquiries are usually short and to the point. "Yes." "No." "I don't know." Rarely do they initiate conversation or ask questions. That's okay. I remind myself that this time is about *them*, not me. Carolyn says I'm rarely at loss for words anyway. Whatever. My purpose in all of this is to take these gentle, challenged souls for a brief getaway that, in turn, might take them back down memory lane.

Sometimes these folks know exactly what they want to eat, and they'll tell me right away. One gal insisted on pizza. So, pizza it was! One fellow wanted chicken, dark meat only. We found that.

Then there was sweet Rosemarie. She hardly talked, but I could tell she was just enjoying the ride. As we waited for our sandwiches, I told her I thought she had a beautiful name. She just smiled. Then a thought came to me. "Rosemarie, do you remember that oldies song from way back? 'Smile a Little Smile for Me'? Your name's in there." She wasn't sure, so I pulled it up on my trusty cell phone and softly played that 1969 song for her right then and there, right at our lunch table. When it got to the chorus, I watched her mouth the words perfectly over and over again. Though no words were spoken at the end of the song, Rosemarie looked up and smiled a little smile for me. That's why I do this.

I've taken "Clay" out a couple of times. He doesn't know how old he is, but he was born in 1954. He played sports in school but can't remember what position or even what school he attended. But you know what? He knows Jesus, and he'll immediately ask you if *you* do. I was asked several times during our outing, and I always responded, "Yes, Clay, I do, and I'm glad you do, too." At lunch last month, I said grace over our meal and felt especially grateful. I was thinking, *Here I am, four years older than this guy, and I'm chauffeuring him around. How blessed I am!* As we were finishing our meal, a lady from a nearby table discreetly bent down on her way out and slipped a $20 bill to the side of my plate, then said, "I see what you're doing. The lunch is on me." Once again, blessed.

Clay and I took a short drive around town and then went up by the Texas Amphitheater as we made our way back to his place. I had an oldies CD playing in the background, which is something I always try to do to lighten the mood. All of a sudden, Clay started patting his knee to the beat of the music. Without saying a word, I glanced over and reflexively just started patting my own knee. When the song finished, Clay extended his hand to me, and we shook hands. We had connected. He asked me again if I knew Jesus. Admiring his boldness and sincerity, I could only smile and say, "I sure do, Clay."

As I walked him into his place, he said to me, "I like you. You're a good man," and I felt honored.

As I made my way back to my Mustang, and to the freedom it gives me, I turned back to Clay and saw him wave goodbye and say, "God Bless You." He already had.

Addendum: In November 2020 (one year to the month when this original article was first published), Clay met Jesus face to face for the first time. What a special day in heaven that was! I was the better person for having met Clay.

8
WHEN FATHERS BECOME HEROES

As I watch my four young grandsons grow up (ages six, three, and one), I find myself observing my son and the way he is with them. I also feel that I'm subconsciously reliving my days as a dad. My goodness, where did the time go? When I was parenting my son and daughter as they were growing up, I tried to incorporate my parents' best parental qualities into my parenting style. I feel like my son, Charles IV, is doing that, as well. It's gratifying for me to see that he coaches Chaz's (his oldest son) basketball team similar to how I coached his teams way back when. He's an encourager, not a screamer. An edifier instead of a criticizer. He's teaching the kids to just have fun and play the game, and he's showing each of them how to be a good sport and an unselfish teammate. I recently told my son that for the next few years, his boys would look up to him not only as a father figure but also as a hero.

I can very well remember the time my own dad became my hero. I was six years old, and the family had gone to Possum Kingdom Lake for a summer outing. I had gone fishing and had put my baited hook between the cracks in the floor of the boat dock. Sure enough, I caught a big bass. But how in the world was I supposed to reel in that whopper through the dock flooring? (Normal six-years-olds don't think of those things in advance). Daddy to the rescue! He quickly surveyed the situation.

Tossing modesty aside, he stripped down to his boxer shorts (in front of everyone; drastic situations call for drastic measures!), jumped into the water, swam under the dock, cut and secured the line in his hand, and emerged with a fish in tow. It was the biggest fish I've ever caught. A six-pound bass for a six-year-old, and it was worthy of a picture in the *Odessa American* newspaper. I was definitely mighty proud of that bass, but I was even more proud of my dad, my hero.

When I told my son that his boys would see him as their "hero" for a season, I also told him that it is very special and that it's the way it's meant to be. However, I also told him that these times are fleeting, as most likely, in the coming few years of adolescence and young adulthood, things will change. There will be big challenges ahead, and my son will be challenged. But through the parental foundation that he and his wife are laying down, and through perseverance, prayer, family support, and counsel, he will get through those turbulent times. Mistakes will be made, and he won't be perfect. Neither was I, and neither was my dad. But the good Lord and the good Book will be his strength and guide. Then, Lord willing, that newborn baby he once held in his arms will again hold him in high esteem. And within a decade or two, his son will become his friend, admirer, and confidant. That's also the way it's meant to be.

Recently, I heard a song called "My Dad," which is by a guy named Paul Petersen, on "oldies" radio. He actually sang that song for his "dad" on *The Donna Reed Show*. As I listened to it, I couldn't help but tear up because it made me think about my own father, and my son, too. Google it and check it out. Some might think songs like this are way too "old-fashioned," but I say that having respect and love for one's father, and telling him about that love and respect, never goes out of style.

When I was at lunch with Charles in Ft. Worth recently, as we stood up to leave the table, my son said to me, "I don't think we've ever been closer." What gratifying words to hear. I did my job.

9
LITTLE DECISIONS MAKE BIG IMPACT

With the local musical drama *The Promise* winding down from its thirtieth season, it takes me back to 1996, when we were relative newcomers to the community. Wife Carolyn and I were excited to live in a small town that had such a big, professional production like *The Promise* happening right there. How special! We got to thinking that maybe our ten-year-old son, Charles, who had some acting and singing experience in church and school (in Tennessee, where we lived the year before we moved to Glen Rose), would like to try out for a part in *The Promise*. We thought he'd be good at this and that it would be right up his alley. Carolyn and I asked him if he'd like to audition. In particular, we thought he might play the role of one of the grandchildren in the family unit who helps narrate the Gospel story. And maybe if he got the part, we thought, Carolyn, our daughter, Noelle, and I could ride his coattails and land roles ourselves. We could make this a regular weekend family affair. But Charles demurred and said he'd rather play basketball. Oh well.

A few days passed, and with the tryout deadline fast approaching, we encouraged him to reconsider. We told him we needed to know after school that day if he'd be willing to at least audition. We weren't optimistic. So, when we picked him up from school that afternoon, he shocked us by saying, "I'm in. I'm trying out." Whoa ho! Why the change of heart? Well, it was "the lure of the ladies." Actually, one little lady in particular: Nicole. She was trying out. Little did we know that our young son's decision would have such wonderful, long-term ramifications and would set a whole set of life-changing events in motion...altering the course of our family's lives to this day.

He and Nicole (and her sister, Renee) did get parts. Carolyn and our daughter, Noelle, sung their way through auditions and were selected, and my meager attempt at "singing" (imagine Barney Fife in the choir) landed me a spot as a ticket taker and usher. For years to come, our family was privileged to be part of something much bigger and greater than ourselves. Powerful, fun, and anecdotal memories abound. How many families have the opportunity to spend five weekends of each year singing and acting out The Greatest Story Ever Told before thousands of people? And all the while, we were hearing and learning about the Scripture and God's ways so that we could apply everything to our own lives. Our eight-year-old daughter was even baptized at *The Promise* on what would have been her grandmother's seventy-third birthday.

My dad, who was very stubbornly reluctant to attend *The Promise* because "he'd seen those types of pageants before," was befriended and loved by cast members. They knew their primary role in all of this was not to be actors and singers on a stage; they were there as ambassadors for Christ. My dad became Odessa's greatest spokesperson for *The Promise* and regularly recruited folks from all over West Texas to attend. People accompanied my dad to see "the pageant" for years. My dad's been gone now for eleven years, and per his request, some of his ashes (and Mom's) are scattered on the grounds of the Texas Amphitheater, where *The Promise* was performed.

In the fall of 2007, our son was off to college, but he came back to Glen Rose for the October weekend when we were holding his grandad's memorial service. He'd also come back because some of his mutual friends from *The Promise* told him about a special gal in the show, and they were going to introduce him to her. "The lure of the ladies" beckoned once again. This time, her name was Leigh. They did meet, and they clicked. Within two years, they were exchanging promises and vows. Charles and Leigh have four children now, and their quiver is full. All boys! Just to think, all of this was because of a fourth grader's decision one day at school, and God's providence.

P.S. I did actually get on stage that one time. The cast was short of male "crowds people." So, duty called, and I was promoted to a full-fledged cast member. There was one stipulation from the director, though: no singing on my part — only miming.

Son Charles in various roles in "The Promise."

10
FITTING NAME FOR A FELLOW I KNOW

Occasionally, when I'm out frequenting a local retail outlet or restaurant, I come across employees who have some type of obvious physical disability or mental challenge. The people's conditions could be congenital or possibly from an accident of some sort; regardless, my heart and admiration immediately goes out to them. I guess I've just always felt that way. When I was a kid, my parents must have taught me to treat people kindly and to be especially respectful to those who face challenges in life that most of us can hardly imagine. I'm particularly moved when I observe these folks just going about their business as if all is "normal." They're just living life, and in many cases, in their worlds, life *is* normal.

It was sometime last fall when I stopped at a fast-food place in a neighboring community and encountered a young man named Justice. Justice had been born with arthrogryposis, a condition which caused severe joint contracture in two to three areas of his body, which, in turn, resulted in abnormal muscle fibrosis and the shortening of and restriction of his arms and legs. You know what, though? He got along just fine. I watched him do his job as he interacted with customers, took food orders, refilled drinks, and cleaned tables. All of this was done with a smile and a work ethic that would make any employer proud. I thought, *Good for him, and good for this eatery!* This establishment had given a chance/job to a guy who had been born into this world with a severe handicap. It made me want to patronize such a place all the more.

Over the last several months, I've had the opportunity to get to know Justice some. Recently, while on a break, I visited with him for a few minutes, and he told me things. I was careful to be very sensitive and gentle in my queries. Justice is in his early twenties and doesn't consider himself someone who has a "disability." He's just someone who has some inconveniences and limitations while doing certain things, but he learned early on to accept, adjust, and get along just fine, "thank you." Heck, he's been that way all of his life and knows no different. With the help of his folks and siblings while he was growing up, he learned to cope with these challenges and just move on with his life. He moves around pretty good, too. He played T-Ball as a youngster and got pretty good at shooting a basketball in his early teens. He does admit that he's stubborn, so much so that when someone says, "Oh, you can't do that," he takes it as a personal challenge to just go out and "do that." His parents were told at birth that he would never walk, but by age two he was getting around with a special walker and small crutches. Know what else? He can hold his breath for up to four minutes. Can you? Me neither.

I've tried to put myself in Justice's shoes and have wondered what my attitude in life would be like had I been faced with similar circumstances. Though I did not ask these questions of him, I've wondered if he's ever wished he could have been a football star or a great track runner. Has he ever wondered if some girl will possibly like him someday in that special way? Has he ever dreamed of playing guitar or piano? I don't know. But I do know this: Justice is an overcomer. Good parenting and family support taught him not to feel sorry for himself, so he chose *not* to.

Throughout all of his schooling, classmates just accepted Justice for who he is: a really good friend. He only remembers one occasion when he was picked on and teased about his condition by a fellow student. How'd that turn out? Well, let's just say that that thirteen-year-old little bully got to find out what a broken nose felt like! Justice served.

Justice believes that in most ways he's pretty much just like everyone else. He has goals and dreams, he has struggles here and there, and he doesn't conform to the norm in all things. I mean, he believes the earth is flat. Really. Hey, that's okay. If we all believed the same things about all things, what fun would that be? I say that diversity is what makes the world go 'round!

I asked one of his supervisors what her thoughts were on having Justice as an employee, and she said, "Oh, everybody here loves Justice. We're very proud to have him as part of our team."

This whole experience of getting to know Justice reminds me of what noted pastor/author Charles Swindoll once said: "I am convinced that life is 10% of what happens to you and 90% of how we react to it. We are in charge of our attitudes." I'd say Justice prevails once again.

11
EXPECT THE UNEXPECTED AT SCHOOL REUNIONS

A few months back, I attended my fifty-year high school reunion out in Odessa. Over the years, I've attended a number of past reunions, so I pretty much knew what to expect, and I looked forward to catching up with old classmates and sharing stories, laughs, and sentimental moments along the way. Embellishing old anecdotes that we've told so many times before makes for heartier laughs and all the more fun. But this reunion was different. Fifty years. How could it be? For a number of us, there seemed to be an underlying, unspoken realization that this might be it; that might have been our last opportunity to see some of the folks who had been such a large part of our pasts.

Upon reflection, there were actually a few unexpected highlights from the event that made it even more memorable. First, there was Becky's mom, Kay. (I wrote about Becky being everybody's favorite in an earlier chapter, and that had been publisher in our local newspaper. She unfortunately passed away from cancer in 1988.) Little did I know that Becky's mom was still alive, residing in Odessa and still getting around a little. Circumstances led to me meeting her, visit a while, and even having lunch together a few days later. What a delightful time it was! After lunch, as I helped her get to the car with her walker, Kay said, "Charlie, your article about Becky was about the nicest thing that's happened to me in a long, long time. I've read it over and over, and it brings me to tears every time. I can't thank you enough."

I leaned over and embraced this ninety-five-year-old lady, and all I could muster up through my own tears was, "You're so welcome." Then it hit me, and the words just came: "I now know, Kay, that I didn't write the story about Becky for the *Glen Rose Reporter*, or even for our classmates at the reunion so much. I wrote it for *you*, and it was a privilege."

Also at the reunion was a guy named Ronnie, whom I did not know well at all. He came up to me and said he thought I had done a really good job as editor of our school newspaper, and he said he admired me for my work on the student council. I had no idea. In school, he and I had talked maybe twice in passing. We just ran in different circles. Ronnie had been a two-year starter for our basketball team, and I had always been a little envious of his athletic prowess. He now lived in the DFW area, and we agreed to do lunch sometime. That did happen a couple of months later, and boy, did we have fun exchanging stories about our high school days. He reiterated that he admired my involvement in student government. Then I said, "Well, as nice as that is for you to say, I wanted to be *you*! Top dog on the BB court!" And I cheerfully added, in jest, that one of OHS's favorite cheerleaders asking him to be her date and escort her to all the homecoming festivities and dance had *no* bearing whatsoever on my, and all of the fellas', envy. Ha!

Finally, there was George. I hadn't seen this classmate in over fifty years. I knew him from junior high. He now lived in Houston and had had to deal with some health problems and other tough issues. I told him I lived in Glen Rose, and he blurted out, "My dad just moved to a nursing home/rehab center in Glen Rose."

Whoa! Why there of all places? I mean, little ol' Glen Rose has only about 2,200 folks, and rural Somervell County is the second smallest county in Texas (it was a good logistical location for all three grown children).

So, when I got back to Glen Rose, I felt led to look up George, Sr. and try to be a friend to my friend's dad. Part of the dwindling "Greatest Generation," George Sr. can still hold a good conversation at age ninety-five, and we've enjoyed talking about "Odessa" things from back in the day. His accounts of the D-Day invasion, which he was involved in, and of marching through France and Germany during WWII are riveting. It makes me appreciate the sacrifices he and my parents' generation made, so that I had the freedom and opportunity to go to high school reunions and grow up in the best of times.

12
TRADING FOOTBALL CLEATS FOR DANCING SHOES

In Odessa, everybody knows football reigns supreme. I can still recall being around five or six years old, sitting between my mom and dad and watching my beloved Odessa High Bronchos take the field against some visiting team from out of town. I just loved the pageantry, the colors, the band, the competition, and the game. And of course, later, when puberty rolled around, I also liked the cheerleaders all decked out in their spiffy red-and-white uniforms. Mainly, though, I just enjoyed being with my parents. Even today, when I get a whiff of cigar smoke, it reminds me of ol' Chunky Hendricks (my parents' good friend who sat in the row in front of us) lighting up his old stogies throughout the game. I guess smoking those things was his way of ridding himself of nervous energy. For me they're just fond memories.

It was a few years later, when I was seven or eight, when my mom asked me if I might like to take ballroom dance lessons. She was met with, "Oh, Mom, dancing's for sissies!" I mean, it was my own mother who used to sing along with the tune of the day: "You've got be a football hero, to get along with a beautiful girl." Well, that was where I was headed. Maybe she knew that a sixth grader who was four feet one and seventy pounds wasn't exactly destined for gridiron heroics. Whatever. I was a little perplexed one day

Tito and Marjorie Montilla

when Mom picked me up from school and headed in the opposite direction of our house. The next thing I knew, we pulled up in front of a place I'd never noticed before. The marquee outside said *Montilla's Ballroom: Dancing for the Young and the Young at Heart*. Uh oh. I sensed that this was not going to be good. She escorted me in there so I could meet Marjorie Montilla, who was one of the dance instructors. Her husband, Tito, was the other.

Marjorie greeted me warmly and then started telling me things they did during the various dance classes. I just sat there. She said, "In our classes, we learn the foxtrot, the cha-cha-cha, and, everybody's favorite, the jitterbug. You like girls, Charlie?"

I uttered an unenthusiastic "Yes, ma'am."

"Well, you just get yourself a'ready because your world is a'fixin' to change. There's about twice as many girls as boys who are taking lessons here. *And* we've even got one variation of the jitterbug where you'll get to dance with two girls at the same time! How would you like that?" By this time, my demeanor had begun its transformation. Mrs. Montilla continued, saying, "We'll have dance parties, cookouts, and live stage performances at the Scott Theater, and then at the end of our ten-week session, we'll have a grand gala celebration so we can show off all we've learned together. How does this sound, Charlie?"

Sign me up. This was where I was headed! This was my first exposure to any type of "culture" outside of the West Texas ways of football and sports. For over three years, I took lessons and learned much more than how to scoot around a dance floor. I was taught the appropriate manner for going through a receiving line and the proper etiquette for asking a girl for a dance, and I learned why it was a good thing to invite a girl to dance when no other boy would. These were some of the social graces I was learning, and they gave me a confidence far beyond my adolescent years.

A couple of decades later, at my twenty-five-year high school reunion, one gal came up to me and introduced her husband to me, saying, "Paul, I'd like you to meet Charlie. Just so you know, he was the best dancer in school." I'd never thought of myself that way. It caught me totally by surprise.

Then, fast-forward another twenty-five years or so to last summer, and there I was with Carolyn. We were attending the musical *Always... Patsy Cline* at the Plaza Theater in Cleburne. It happened again. We were sitting there enjoying the show when, about halfway through the performance, there came "Louise" (one of the two main characters). She was dashing up the aisle, and out of all the people there, she pointed directly at me and said, "Come with me, big boy. You're my partner for this dance!" Oh my, it was totally unexpected! Before I even had time to think, I was down there, front and center, waltzing away with the star of the show in front of around three hundred folks. I was not perfect by any means, but I was able to hold my own as I held her in my arms. Whew! I was sorta glad when it was over, but still.

Then, a couple of months ago, an older lady who was sitting behind us at church just out of the blue said to me during greeting time, "I saw you dance at the Plaza Theater. Not bad for a Baptist!"

Although I exchanged football cleats for dancing shoes, I still got along with a pretty gal, and I married Carolyn thirty-eight years ago.

Not even knowing I was "in my element"...front left with pretty girl.

13
DELIVERANCE DAY CELEBRATED EACH YEAR

Ten years ago, I almost lost my daughter. I was in my Kansas City hotel room when I received a call from my wife at about 6:45 p.m. Speaking with panicky, short breaths, she told me that Noelle (college sophomore at Stephen F. Austin State University in Nacogdoches) had been struck by an out-of-control pickup truck as she walked along a campus sidewalk after band practice. It seemed as if the driver of the truck, Chris (a senior at SFA), had been careening down College Avenue, glancing off cars (his brakes had failed) suddenly veered right, jumped the curb, and hit my daughter. Within a split second, he'd also knocked down a forty-foot light pole (which landed less than ten feet from my daughter) and come to a smashing halt on a grassy embankment. Neither Chris, his passenger, nor any other pedestrians were injured. Further details were sketchy, but Carolyn was supposed to call me back as soon as she heard more from the SFA band director.

I felt like I'd been literally kicked in the stomach. So, for about twenty minutes, life itself seemed to be put on hold. I wondered if it was all just a bad, bad dream. Did I really hear what I thought I just heard? I fell on my knees, praying, crying, and pleading with God to spare my daughter. "Please, dear God, if it be within Your will, just take me, not my sweet

Noelle." Instinctively, I called a few close friends and solicited their prayers.

I was praying on the phone with Bobby when my wife called back with the good news! Though Noelle had a dislocated hip, torn ligaments in her left knee, and significant abrasions and contusions to her torso, limbs, and scalp, these injuries were *not* life-threatening. Vital signs were good, and there was no spinal injury, nor were there significant facial cuts. I wept with gratitude and thanked my Creator, the giver of life itself.

The good Lord had provided a guardian angel that day: fellow bandmate Freddie Lopez. While walking alongside her on that sidewalk, he had looked up and seen the pickup barreling its way toward them. He had the presence of mind to quickly grab her elbow and sharply yank her to his left, directly out of the path of the pickup. Instead of being run over, she had been sideswiped. How I thanked God for Freddie!

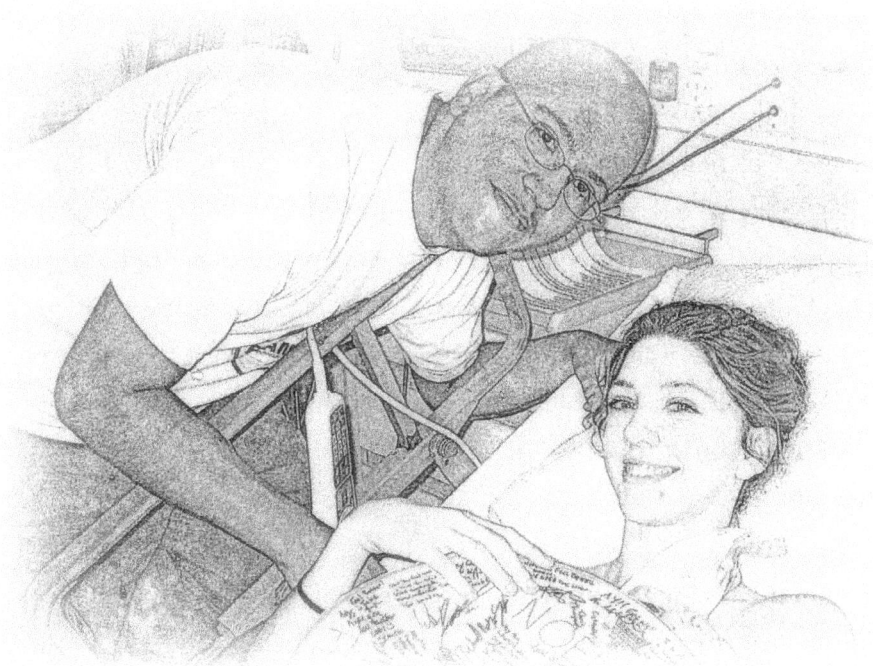

Though it took only months for Noelle to recover physically (after having ACL surgery on the knee), it took quite a bit longer both emotionally and psychologically. But spiritually, the impact was immediate. Perspectives on life and what's really important were changed in an instant for the Norman family. I remember writing out the check for her surgery and thinking that whatever the amount — $1,000, $10,000, or all of the money I had — it mattered not, as I still had Noelle.

Understandably, Chris and Noelle never had any contact. As time passed and healing took place, Noelle did wonder more about the accident and knew only Chris had the answers. She also thought that if she could somehow meet him, she could tell him that all was okay and that some good had come from the accident. During graduation week in May of 2011, she worked up the nerve to go over to where Chris supposedly lived, only to find out that he'd moved to Wisconsin two years earlier. Oh well.

In the fall of 2012, Carolyn and I went down to Nacogdoches to be with Noelle (she was still working in the area) and watch her fiancé play in the annual SFA alumni rugby match. During the game, Noelle happened to notice a guy in the crowd who looked just like Chris (she'd seen Facebook photos). It *was* him! Noelle was brave that day. With a prayer on her lips and forgiveness in her heart, she reached out to the guy who had almost taken her life. They talked for maybe twenty minutes. She asked questions she'd had since that fateful day. But even more importantly, she told Chris about how her life had been changed for the good because of the accident. She told him that she was now more committed to the Lord than ever before, that she now appreciated each day she was given, and that she forgave him. This divine time with Chris provided a sense of closure for this chapter of her life.

On August 23rd, we'll again celebrate Noelle's "Deliverance Day" and remember this time-tested adage: Yesterday is history, tomorrow is a mystery, and today is a gift. That's why it's called "the present."

P.S. Who could ever have imagined that exactly ten years to the day of the accident, my Noelle would be hiking the Appalachian Trail with her husband of four years? Only He could.

14

MORE THAN I BARGAINED FOR

People who know me well know that two of my great interests in life are history and football. In particular, the American Civil War, WWII, college football, and the stadiums and venues in which college games are played. As a result, a few years back, I ventured to Oxford, MS, so I could check out the campus of the University of Mississippi (Ole Miss), learn more about the history of the school, and try to see if I could get inside the Ole Miss stadium to view the football field.

Some fifty-eight years ago, Ole Miss was the epicenter of racial conflict and violence because of school integration and segregation in our country. In September of 1962, the all-white school denied admission to James Meredith (a US Air Force veteran) upon discovering he was African American. Meredith was a junior who had met the academic qualifications as a transfer student from Jackson State University, and he wanted to obtain a degree from the state's flagship university. Thus, he pressed on. Major controversy and upheaval ensued, and there were national ramifications. Despite receiving death threats, Meredith did not back down. Neither did campus officials, and neither did Ross Barnett, the governor of Mississippi at that time. That is, until President Kennedy and his administration intervened and basically forced the school to admit Meredith. Thousands on campus rioted throughout the night. Two people were killed, and over three hundred were injured. The US Marshals and the National Guard were called in to quell the uprising. Meredith *was* admitted, and he graduated from there in August of 1963. He paved the way for racial integration at institutes of higher learning across our country.

So, there I was, standing next to the Lyceum, the university's administration building, which was built in 1848 and was the site of these riots. Approximately fifty feet away was the life-size statue of James Meredith, along with an appropriate plaque that marked the significance of the time and place. As I was taking in the moment, I wondered if I might be able to find someone who would take my picture with the Lyceum. About that time, a sharply dressed, middle-aged black man who was wearing an Ole Miss polo shirt came walking by, and I asked him if he would mind taking my picture while I stood at the entrance of the Lyceum. "Not at all," he said.

We exchanged pleasantries, and before I knew it, he asked me if I'd like to take a short tour of the building. "I can take you," he said.

The next thing I knew, this gentleman was walking me through halls of history. I felt a strange sense of pride, guilt, patriotism, and justice when I noticed that folks of all backgrounds and races were glancing up from their desks and workplaces, smiling and acknowledging my guide and me. It was as if my guide was saying to the office workers, "He's with me." I could not help but think of the irony of the situation: This man of color was escorting *me* around the site he would not have been welcome at fifty-five years earlier.

He told me that the Lyceum had once served as a hospital for both Confederate and Union soldiers during the Civil War, and that when the Union overtook the rebels in Oxford, General Ulysses S. Grant rode his horse through the hallways of the building . He showed me the office where James Meredith signed papers for his admission into the university in 1962. He took me into the north parlor room, where there were extravagant wallpaper murals that depicted colonial-era scenes of America the beautiful, all of them visualized and painted by French artists in the 1840s, though they had never even been to America (Niagara Falls, Boston Harbor, West Point, etc.). And beautiful it was! Then my host led me to an adjoining room and said, "Now, this is the chancellor's office. Would you like to sit behind his desk? I'll take your picture." WOW! Would I? And I did.

He then escorted me outside and pointed to the site where those all-night riots had taken place that dark September night in 1962. After pausing briefly and smiling, he pointed to another area, saying, "We affectionately call this 'the Grove.' It's where we have our famous tailgate parties before our football games. We have a saying here at Ole Miss: We might lose a football game, but we never, *ever* lose a tailgate!" We both smiled.

Then it was time to go. My gracious escort had an appointment with a professor that he needed to keep. After pausing briefly, I looked this man straight in the eye and thanked him, and after giving him a firm handshake, I said, "I'm glad you're here."

"Yeah, me, too."

By the way, within ten minutes, I was having my picture taken as I kneeled on the sideline of the 65,000-seat Vaught Hemingway Stadium. Somehow, it all seemed a little anticlimactic. Maybe you understand. Go Rebs!

15

THE RING THAT WAS NEVER LOST

When I heard of the passing of ninety-six-year-old, famed Texas jeweler James Avery last month, it took me back to a time when the hand of Providence had reached down and touched me in a way I'll never forget. Some twenty year ago, I had the privilege of sharing this true story with Mr. Avery in person, and so today I will share it with you.

Back in 1971, between my junior and senior years at Texas Tech, I had the wonderful opportunity to travel to and work in Hawaii for the summer with several fellow college students. Before I left on my trip, my mother gave me a small, sterling-silver "Christian" ring to wear. Simplistic in design, its centered cross cut out, this style of ring later became a signature example of James Avery's quality craftsmanship. I wore this ring, not because I was particularly "religious," but because it was a gift from my mom, and I liked the look. One day that summer, I lost my ring while tossing a football with friends on Waikiki Beach. When I returned home to finish up school at Tech, my mom gave me another ring just like the one I'd lost on the beach, and I wore that ring for the rest of my college years and beyond.

Though I considered myself a "pretty good Christian" — I had been raised in church, I believed in God, and I had been baptized — I really wasn't very interested in spiritual things. However, after a series of events, and after I got to know a few specific people over the next couple of years, I realized there was definitely something missing in my life. These new friends were on a completely different spiritual level than I was. They told me that the difference in their lives was a personal relationship with Jesus Christ. That actually sounded a little "foreign" to me. Though I had been a somewhat faithful church member while growing up, this idea of a "personal relationship" made me feel a bit uncomfortable (may I say convicted?). Either way, I could tell they were speaking truth to me. I knew that God loved me and had a plan for my life. Still, I was not interested. Yet I realized that I certainly did not have the peace, direction, or purpose in life that these people possessed. They weren't talking about joining a denomination or religion or giving to a cause; they were talking about a life change that required me to commit my life to the One who made me and knew all about me.

After a few weeks of struggling with pride, selfishness, and other issues, in October of 1972, I got down on my knees in my Austin, TX, apartment and said to God, "If You are really real, please forgive me, change me, and take control of my life, dear Lord. I accept you, Jesus, as my Lord and Savior." Shortly thereafter, things did begin to change for me. I had new goals, perspectives, and priorities. I was liking the "new me" better, too. And the ring I wore...well, it had an added significance because of my newfound faith.

After finishing up grad school at UT, of all things, I got a job to return to Hawaii. I worked in advertising for Honolulu's two daily newspapers. After a few weeks there, I met a young lady named Sandy, who worked at one of the ad agencies I called on. She told me that she, too, had recently moved back to the islands after having lived in Arizona for a couple of years. Sandy then noticed my ring and asked me about it. I told her I wore it because I was a Christian. She said that she had recently become interested in spiritual things, as well, so I invited her to come to church with me sometime. She accepted my invitation, and the first Sunday we went together, she went forward and committed her life to the Lord. (Well, that was easy!)

Sandy and I got closer over time, and we did things together on occasion. One special evening, she joined me for a covered-dish dinner, a Bible study, and fellowship in Manoa Valley. During the meal, Sandy came over to sit next to me and casually said, "Did I ever tell you that I had a ring like the one you have?"

"No, don't think so. Where did you get it?" I replied.

"You remember that I used to live in Hawaii a few years ago, like you? Well, this couple were friends of mine, and they found a ring like yours on the beach and gave it to me."

It took a few seconds for my mind to process this. Then I inquired some more, saying, "Now, when and where was this?"

"Let's see, it was the summer of 1971, and it was on Waikiki Beach."

I was taken aback for a moment while my thoughts raced back to the time when I had lost my first ring on that beach. She told me she had kept the ring in a jewelry drawer in her apartment. Later that night, I slipped on *the very ring* that I had lost on the ocean's shore three years earlier. We stood there in silent awe. What were the odds? Upon hearing my story, a statistics professor at the University of Hawaii told me the chances of this happening were "infinitesimally small."

Already, I had begun to understand that I serve a sovereign God who orchestrates people and circumstances in ways that serve His purposes. He had chosen to reveal His omnipotence to His new followers, Sandy and me, by showing us that He knew us as individuals, that he knew exactly where we were, that He worked in tangible ways, and that He could intervene for us and bring about situations and relationships that would build our faith and trust in Him.

Sandy and I remain friends to this day. Carolyn and I have visited her and her husband, Dale, in their home in Maryland. She has her ring, and I have mine. Our ring story is a testimony of our Creator's wondrous ways, and it shows that He knows and cares about every detail of our lives. It's my greatest privilege to be a child of the King. Believing in miracles comes with being part of the family.

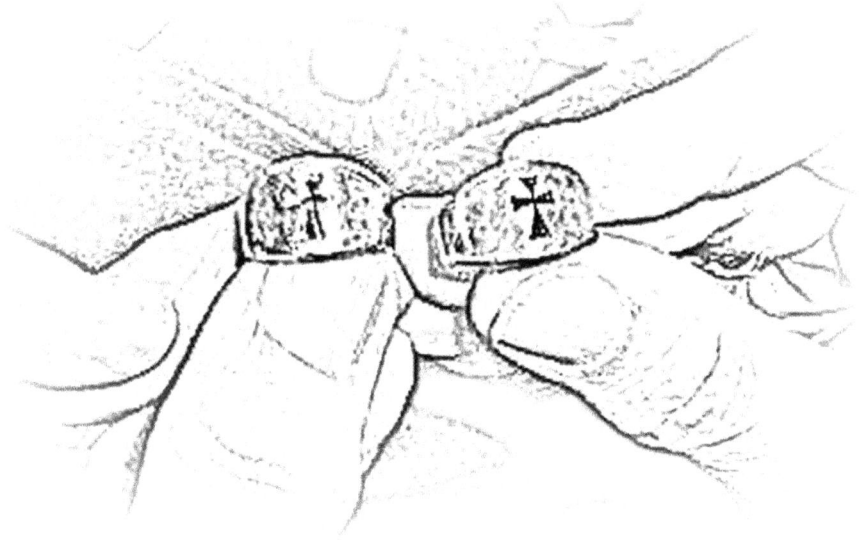

16
LET THE HEALING BEGIN

Seventy-seven years ago, our country was thrust into World War II when Japanese Naval and Air Forces attacked our Naval base at Pearl Harbor in Hawaii. Known as Pearl Harbor Day, over 2,300 Americans died in the attack. This could be considered my generation's 9/11, and like 9/11, the lives of all Americans were put on hold.

My dad had to leave college (never to return) to join the military. He ended up in the Army Air Corps and was shipped off to the South Pacific to fight the Japanese. It was a bitter struggle, and there were lingering consequences for him and thousands of other survivors of the war. Though my dad hardly spoke of his experience in the military, while growing up, I sensed that he had an inner (maybe subconscious) resentment toward anything Japanese. I'd hear the occasional derogatory ethnic slur during conversations, and I just knew.

Many years later, after I graduated college in 1974, I had the wonderful opportunity to work and live in Hawaii for a time. One of my fellow co-workers was a man my dad's age. His name was Tadao, and he was an American of Japanese descent. For some reason, we just took a liking to each other and bonded quickly. A man of small stature, Tadao was meek, kind, and very smart, and he took great pleasure in showing me the ways

Japanese culture had become part of the Hawaiian way of life. He introduced me to certain Japanese delicacies, and later I sipped "saké" (rice wine) for the first time at a Japanese-Hawaiian family gathering. I reciprocated by taking him to Mama's Mexican Kitchen and introducing him to tacos and enchiladas. Not exactly Tex-Mex, but not bad.

It's wasn't until later that I discovered that Tadao himself had been imprisoned by the US government in Hawaii right after Pearl Harbor. The reason: He was of Japanese lineage. Months later, after thorough vetting, he was released from internment and became an interpreter/translator for the US Military in Honolulu. I never sensed that he felt any animus toward America because he had been incarcerated.

Upon my invitation, my parents came to visit me on the islands for about a week, and I loved showing them around Oahu (Waikiki Beach, Diamond Head Crater, and, of course, Pearl Harbor and the Arizona Memorial). I also wanted them to meet some of my special friends, including Tadao. Earlier, I had asked Tadao if he'd be willing to help prepare an authentic Japanese dinner (complete with a tatami floor and a low table) for me and my folks. He said that he'd be delighted and that he'd make all of the arrangements. All we had to do was "show up" at the hotel, and he'd escort us to the penthouse restaurant for a private dinner. I had given my parents a little background on Tadao and my idea, and they agreed to go. I do admit that I was a little uncertain about how it'd all work out. I only recalled my dad conversing with Asian Americans during times when the family had driven from Odessa to Midland, TX, to eat Chinese at the Blue Star Inn, and he'd "quiz" the waiters on the various menu items.

Well, the big night came, and as we drove up to the hotel, we spotted Tadao. He was standing by the curb, waiting to greet my mom and dad, along with me and my date. Upon introduction, Tadao bowed slightly in respect and deference, first to my mom and then to my dad, and then gently placed a beautiful Hawaiian lei around each of our necks (made especially for us by his wife, specifically for this occasion). It was one of those fleeting moments when I knew something special had just happened. For my dad, the ugly scar of bitterness and unforgiveness was being soothed by the sweet, healing balm of respect and humility. Bitterness had begun to give way to betterment.

Well, dinner and the ensuing conversations throughout the evening could not have gone better. In his soft Japanese-Hawaiian accent, Tadoa personally ordered and explained all of the various foods for us — everything from pickled squid to seaweed salad. We knew that Tadao felt honored to share his lifestyle with us, which was far removed from our West Texas ways. We topped it all off with a toast to new friends.

I not only savored the pleasing aftertaste of the meal we'd just shared, but even more so, I also savored the change that was beginning to take place in my daddy's heart. While full manifestation was still years away, I knew the good Lord was doing work on/in my father. I knew there had been a breakthrough when, around 1990, after having only loved Fords and Chevrolets over the years, he bought a Toyota (Camry) for the first time, and he became a Toyota man for the rest of his life. I feel privileged to have been there for the transformation.

17

NO MORE PROBLEMS WITH "ACOUSTICS"

I traveled to Odessa this past month for a high school reunion, and it took me back to when I had my first real "paying" job. I was a sixteen-year-old whippersnapper who was hired to be a part-time summer tour guide for The Globe of the Great Southwest, the most authentic replica (at the time) of William Shakespeare's original sixteenth-century Globe Theatre in London.

The original Globe first opened in 1599 on the banks of the River Thames, and it was the venue for the debuts of a number of Shakespeare's plays. In the mid-1960s, in an effort to share another type of culture with West Texans, high school English teacher (a friend of my mom's; later a professor at Odessa College) Majorie Morris started an area-wide project that involved researching, raising funds, and building an octagon-shaped two-story structure that was fashioned after the original Globe in England. It would serve as a place for local community arts and theater performances (and the annual Shakespeare festival), and it would hopefully lure Shakespearian enthusiasts and other tourists to Odessa, as well. Completed in 1968, the replica has 441 seats, a wrap-around/full-view balcony, and an apron-styled stage that only enhances the atmosphere of intimacy that is reminiscent of the Bard's early-1600s London dramas.

So, there I was, all decked out in my Elizabethan-era costume, waiting for interested parties to show up and request a tour. I was just praying that I wouldn't know anyone who came in. I mean, I was a "wannabe" footballer who was now attired in a ruffled, long-sleeved pink shirt; a tight, tapered vest/jacket; and multi-colored trunks (puffy shorts with black hose). And to top it off, I had to don a Shakespearian-style actor hat with a feather on it! Not exactly the image I was hoping to portray as an athlete in the making. But, hey, I *was* making a whopping $1.50 an hour! And on most days, only a handful of people would show up for a tour. On some days, no one came. But I still got paid no matter what. I was beginning to understand (and like) how this "work thing" worked.

One particular day, there was a family of four (a dad, a mom, and a couple of kids) from out of state who showed up and wanted a tour. I took their $5 payment and led them around the theatre, giving them my well-prepared fifteen-minute spiel. All the while, I was pointing out some of the various historical aspects and dimensions of the original Globe, explaining how the one in Odessa measured up quite nicely. We ended our tour in the balcony, and I casually asked if anyone had any questions (like I would know the answer; yeah right). The husband piped up and said, "Yes, I have one. Have you had any trouble with acoustics in the theatre?"

Uh oh. I was not sure what he meant. I hemmed and hawed around. I was thinking, *acoustics? What are acoustics!* Finally, my answer came out as something like this: "Uh, well...uh, no, not really. We, uh, had the place sprayed for 'em last week, and the exterminators assured us right off that the acoustic problem was all taken care of. Everything is just fine and dandy. Yes, siree, Bob. Any more questions?"

"No, I don't think so. We must be going now, kids."

All I know is that the Globe Theater in Odessa must have addressed any concerns with acoustics early on, and the building has had no lingering issues with any such vermin. To this day, The Globe of the Great Southwest is still the venue for Shakespearean and drama performances, community plays, and concerts. All the while, it brings a little touch of European culture and English literature to the oil patch and the good folks of West Texas, just as Majorie intended in the first place. Y'all come back now.

The Globe Theatre of the Great Southwest

18
"PUKI" – BIG DOG IN A LITTLE PACKAGE

Today, I write with a heavy heart. My longtime pet dog and faithful friend "Puki" was killed in an accident yesterday. She was my sweet and loyal companion for fourteen years, and for a pug that's a long, full life. But Puki was a survivor. Over the years, she endured the mange, having an eye pulled out of its socket, a copperhead bite, and heat stroke, and she got lost (and was found miles from home) three times.

Just like humans, she had her quirks and idiosyncrasies: She coughed, scratched, yawned, gagged, snorted, snored, tooted, sneezed, and did not close her mouth when she ate. People do these things, too, but we're sometimes too proud or embarrassed to admit it. Not my "Pukeroo." She just lived life.

Much to Carolyn's chagrin, Puki once devoured a large, gift-wrapped chocolate bar she'd found on the sun room's floor. It had been meant for a friend. Carolyn was definitely not a happy camper. However, I will say (at least in this one instance, anyway) that Puki did not feel guilty at all. She was a little hyper for a day or two (Puki and Carolyn both; just saying).

As dog lovers will attest, many times we wish people would be more like our canine friends — innocent, gentle, transparent, loving, quick to forgive, and without pretense. In all of her years, Puki never, ever bit or snapped at anyone (even a child who innocently pulled her tail).

She patiently sat at my feet some twelve years ago and listened to my first meager attempts at learning how to "sing" and play a song on guitar. My being off-key and out of tune didn't matter to her. She acknowledged my efforts and gave me her devoted attention as well as some doggy kisses. What a friend!

Occasionally I'd give her a chewy treat after dinner and jokingly say to her, "Now, close your mouth when you eat. No smacking!" She'd just unabashedly smack away anyway, much to the annoyance of Carolyn. I think Puki and I both enjoyed those lighthearted moments when she irritated my wife. They always lifted the mood in the moment (to me anyway).

She brought laughs, smiles, and a sense of optimism to all who knew her. I think of my dad, who passed away almost eleven years ago, and how Puki was such sweet therapy to him during the last few years of his life. She was a link to my past, and that's why it hurts so deeply to have her taken so quickly and unexpectedly. To know her was to love her.

I'd like to thank Dr. Gary and Dr. Paul Crabtree (and the wonderful staff at Squaw Valley Veterinary) for their personal, tender care of Puki over the years. And to Puki's pals — Susan and Ken, Chandler, Elena and the girls, Bennie, Weldon, Michael, and the many others — thank you for enjoying our fun little dog with us, and for sharing in our grief. You understand, and that helps.

All that said, there is a much bigger picture to the story. I believe that God made pets and animals for our pleasure and enjoyment. I miss her greatly and am in mourning, so I can hardly fathom what parents go through when losing a child. Carolyn and I came close to that with our son thirteen years ago and then with our daughter two years after that. God, in His great mercy and compassion, spared them. Should things have gone differently, only by His grace could we have carried on. As Scripture reminds us in the first book of Job, "He gives and takes away. Yet I will say 'Blessed be the name of the Lord.'" Only He could have given us the strength to utter those words.

The accident that took Puki from us contains lessons for all of my family. Maybe months, or maybe many years, from now, a tragedy involving a child or some other person will be averted because of what we learned this day. We'll call it "The Puki Principle" in her honor.

I also believe that if the good Lord knows when a sparrow falls from the sky, surely he knows about Puki and the hurt we are now feeling. Because the Bible speaks of wondrous animals in heaven, though we don't yet know what they are, I'm choosing to believe He just might have our beloved pets there as well. With heaven being a place of perfect peace and unspeakable joy, where the lion and the lamb dwell together, which is what the good Book tells us, why not? Being the giver of all good things and one who gives us the desires of our heart, He could grant us a reunion with those special pets that we loved so dearly, the pets that loved us unconditionally. I can just see Puki waiting there for me, her tail wagging, smacking her lips as she holds out an open paw that's full of Hershey's Kisses, ready to share.

19

QUEST FOR A TROPHY

My elementary school in Odessa, Austin Elementary, hadn't had a new trophy for its trophy case in years. Even as an eleven-year-old sixth grader, I felt the burden of being part of a "loser" school, and it hurt. During my last semester there, since I was a "wannabe" athlete who loved sports and competition, I tried out for and made the school's track team. Coach Harrison assigned me and nine other boys to Class F, the last category. It was for boys weighing seventy pounds or less. Coach Harrison selected me to compete in the high jump and to run the third leg of the relay race.

Now, I'd had some practice jumping. I often practiced high jumps by using the pegged stands my Grandfather Norman had made for me a couple of years earlier. In time, I got to be pretty good at "scissor kicking" my way over the crossbar, and on a really good day, I could clear four feet.

Our team had some practice meets early on during the track season, but the big day was the annual citywide track meet at Barrett Stadium, which was for all schools. This was "big time" in my little eyes. I remember walking out on the field that blustery March day in 1962. I was taken aback by the twenty-plus school teams that were all decked out in their school colors. I felt excited, a little intimidated, and somewhat hopeful as the meet began. When it was time for my event and I was preparing to jump, I noticed my dad pushing my wheelchair-bound grandfather to a spot around thirty feet away, where they had a good view (my granddad suffered from Parkinson's disease, among other maladies, and would be gone within two years). In a sense, I was jumping for him as well as my school. Well, I won the event with my jump of four feet. With my score and other class F teammates' scores, Austin Elementary secured enough points to win its first trophy in a decade. I was exhilarated, thrilled, and relieved all at the same time. For the first time in my life, I experienced the deep satisfaction that comes from being part of something much greater than yourself.

After we received the trophy a couple of weeks later, Coach Harrison wrote the names of the ten boys who had contributed to our winning the Class F City Championship on the back of the trophy, then prominently placed it in the display case by the principal's office. How proud I was! Over the next several years, I ventured back to Austin a time or two and saw that trophy again.

Then, back in the early 1990s, when my family was in Odessa visiting my widowed father, I took my teenage son and daughter to the school where I had first learned to read and write, as I wanted to show them the trophy. To my dismay, the trophy case was gone! I inquired about its whereabouts in the office, and the principal said that because of building renovations, the case had been removed. But she thought the trophies had been placed in boxes down in the basement. She summoned the custodian and had him take us there to have a look. Several minutes later, we were all sorting through boxes of old memorabilia, medals, and trophies. Then, there it was! I cradled the trophy in my hands and showed it to Charles and Noelle.

The custodian looked at me and asked, "Would you like to have it? I'm not sure what the school is going to do with all of these trophies, anyway."

"Why yes! I'd be honored."

After getting the principal's blessing, a few minutes later, I walked out of my old school with a cherished token from years ago. I glanced at the names on the back and reminisced a bit, knowing that some of those boys were no longer with us. It sure made me step back and think.

Also, as a grandfather myself now, I've wondered how my own granddad must have felt when he saw his namesake succeed in something he had helped initiate. I think I know.

I sometimes wonder what we're teaching kids today. Now it seems everybody on a team is entitled to a "participation trophy" for just showing up. How special is that? Not very. Are we teaching them that it's good and right to work hard for a common goal and achieve an objective? Not really. Shouldn't we teach them that it's sometime good to lose and face disappointment? Doesn't it teach them to work harder next time? It makes one appreciate the victory all the more. Sort of like life in general. But also, there's the deeper satisfaction of *earning* the reward, especially as a team. Silly and trivial as it may seem, that little trophy — Class F 61-62 Austin — still holds a special place in my heart fifty-seven years later.

20

A MOTHER'S LOVE IS NEVER FORGOTTEN

Last week, my mother would have turned ninety-five. It's hard to believe that she's been gone twenty-three years now. But her influence in my life is ever present and will be with me all of my days.

Minnie Fay (a good ol' southern name that fit my mom to a T) loved to socialize, play cards (especially "bridge"), and just do things spontaneously. She loved to travel and try new things, and I got that from her. Though she was not a college graduate, she wanted me to be, and she wanted me to experience different cultures and ways of life outside of West Texas. When I was in the seventh grade, she told me that when I grew up, she didn't want me to live in Odessa. It wasn't that she didn't like Odessa (she loved Odessa; there were great people, beautiful sunsets, and good schools); she just felt that there was more for me to experience and explore beyond the arid plains of the Permian Basin.

I was an only child, and she sought out different ways she could expose me to "cultural things," such as the time when I was eleven years old and she dragged me to Montilla's dance studio so she could sign me up for ballroom dance lessons. As a "wannabe" football hero, I protested as best as I could, blurting out, "Mom, dancing is for sissies!" That is, until that first lesson, when I realized there were two girls for every boy in class! Mom knows best!

When I was presented with an opportunity to go Europe for six weeks with a group of graduating seniors right out of high school, she immediately said, "You're going." It was a life-changing adventure that set the course for my future career and lifestyle.

My mom was one to share little nuggets of wisdom with anyone who'd listen. Quips like: "You got to love people, warts and all," "The most important things in life aren't things," and "Be sure and take a cookie when the plate is passed."

Most importantly, during the years I was growing up, my mother taught me to have my heart open to spiritual things, which came to fruition later in life. She was the one who first told me that Jesus loves me. She reminded me often that she was praying for me and that God was always in control. Though I did believe in all of that, I went through a disinterested, apathetic phase during my early college years. When pressed about whether I'd attended church one particular Sunday morning, I told her on the phone, "Mom, how could I go to church? I've got the worst hangover I've ever had!" But Mom persisted and taught me by example. For example, she faithfully put $25 in the offering plate every Sunday, even when we didn't have a lot of money. She reminded me that God owns everything we have and that He loves a cheerful giver.

When my mother was diagnosed with terminal cancer at the age of seventy-one, she became an even greater witness of faith to those around her (including my dad and me). She told those who had listening ears that she had no fear of dying, and she said that soon God's angels would be escorting her to her eternal home. She yearned to see Jesus, to be with Jesus, and she took comfort in knowing that she'd see us again on the other side someday.

I was with her when she passed from this life. Kneeling beside her deathbed, I heard her whisper these last sweet, strained words to me: "Charlie, my son, I love you. *You* were the highlight of my life." How does one process those words? I felt honored, humbled, unworthy, and loved. I bowed my head and cried. I missed my momma. It was then that I realized that there's nothing quite like a mother's love for her child, regardless of age, warts and all.

21
GRANDKIDS SEE A DIFFERENT SIDE OF DADDY☺

People who know me really well know that I can be a jokester at times. But my grandkids didn't know this about me. They probably thought of their "Daddy☺" as more of a "fuddy-duddy" than a practical joker. I understood. But on a recent trip to Tennessee with me and Carolyn, my two oldest grandsons became aware of their paternal grandfather's occasional "craziness," and that was a good thing. A good, old-fashioned, harmless practical joke can do the body good and can take relationships to another level. Somehow, the subject came up, and I shared one of my more elaborate jokes from back in the day with them.

It was Thanksgiving week in 1968, and I was a college freshman living in the dorm at Texas Tech. I heard on the radio that a contestant had just won a free turkey (fully cooked and prepared) for the holiday and could pick it up at the station any day that week. Then my mind started clicking ("scheming" might be a better word) I thought, I wonder what someone would do if they won a *live* turkey? Hey, what about a dozen! Yeah, that was it. That could be fun. And I knew just the gal to play this trick on: slightly naïve, sweet-natured Laura! Laura was a good friend of mine from high school in Odessa, and she was also attending Tech. I knew that she just might be gullible enough to fall for this kind of prank if it were done well enough. I got several guys in the dorm in on it, and boy, did we have a fun time brainstorming!

The key to it was Fred, the one guy in our dorm who had a perfect DJ voice. We got our plan together and gathered in the dorm room. Fred called Laura, got her on the phone, and said, "Is this Laura speaking? Well, good afternoon, Laura. This is George Clark from the radio station KLBB (he purposely said the made-up call letters so quickly that it would hard to remember), and I just want to congratulate you for winning our grand prize in our Thanksgiving giveaway! Your name was drawn, and a dozen *live* turkeys from Olsen's Turkey Farm will be delivered to your dorm within twenty-four hours. Congratulations once again, and thanks for listening to Lubbock's number-one station!" Man, did he sound authentic!

Then I persuaded a few mutual friends to call Laura, tell her they'd just heard the news, and ask her what in the world she was going to do with twelve live turkeys. I purposely did not call, but I did receive a call from her a couple of hours later. She wanted to know if I knew anything about all of this. I was intentionally evasive about it; I only said that I had heard the news on the radio, and I congratulated her! Ha! She inquired about what station I had heard it on, and I said I couldn't remember because I listened to several. She told me she had called every radio station in town, and none of them knew anything about it. It was then that I knew we had her.

We knew we couldn't come through with the delivery of a dozen live turkeys, but we also knew we just couldn't leave her empty-handed. So, I went out and bought a dozen extra-large chicken eggs, packaged them just right, and typed out very specific instructions on how to successfully incubate turkey eggs. We printed out a professional-looking cover sheet that expressed the station's sincere apologies for not being able to come through with live turkeys (unexpected surge in demand at the farm?). Our hope was that she would precisely follow the included directions (we wrote things like, keep the eggs exactly one and a half inches apart, heat lamp six inches away and at no more than 115 degrees, etc.) for a few days and that she would believe there was a possibility she could be a proud "mother hen" of a dozen poults within the week.

I discreetly delivered the box to the front desk of her dorm that afternoon, and within two hours I got another call from Laura. She was asking me again if I knew anything about all of this. Who, me? Wonder why she would suspect me? Actually, she knew me pretty well; that was the problem.

But we guys sure had fun visualizing our good friend carefully tending to those eggs for Lord knows how long. I never, ever confessed to this (mis)deed, although over the years, when our paths have crossed on occasion, Laura always brings it up. I just smile innocently. My grandkids would be proud.

22
PROUD TO BE #3

This Sunday, many of us will be celebrating Father's Day. Though my dad passed away around thirteen years ago, I probably think of him at least several times each day. I was privileged to have had him in my life for fifty-seven years. Not everyone is so blessed. Of course, Dad and I had our times. He could be gruff, volatile, profane, extremely stubborn, and, basically, a stick in the mud. There were a couple of occasions when we didn't speak for weeks. But I always loved him.

I think back on times when my dad was my "daddy." He taught me that being physically affectionate with one's kids is not sissy; it's *manly*. He taught me that being a bit early for an appointment was not only being punctual, but it was also being just plain courteous. He taught me to give a firm handshake and to look folks in the eye when speaking to them or being spoken to. He showed me how to tie a tie, how to drive a car, and how to shave around that "Norman Adam's apple." My dad also taught me about sex before I was interested. He wanted me to know things before the other boys started talking.

My dad was a hardened man. He grew up during the Depression and worked the farm the day after school let out for summer until the day before it started up again. He went to war in the Pacific, got severely ill over there, and then came home for an extended hospital stay. Within the next three years, my parents lost a daughter during childbirth (when most friends already had a kid or two).

My father also drank a bit, maybe a little too much on occasion. For the first decade of my life, he went to church with Mom and me, but sometime in the mid-1960s he just stopped going. Though he was "the life of the party" and everybody loved Charlie (senior class favorite in high school), in many ways I did *not* want to be like him. The thing is, at age sixty-nine, I am *a lot* like him.

It's said that it is difficult for an older person to change his or her ways. I tend to agree. However, my father *did* change in the last few years of his life. It started when Mom was diagnosed with terminal colon cancer. He saw how her faith in God sustained her and how she had no fear of dying. He watched the hospice caregivers and the way they were with my mother. The Almighty had filled their tender hearts with love for my sweet, dying mom. As she grew weaker over the ensuing months, Mom and Dad "went to church together" by watching the *Gaither Homecoming Hour* TV show on Saturday nights.

After Mom passed in 1995, and after much persuasion, Dad finally relented and came to Glen Rose to see his grandkids perform in *The Promise*. He was reluctant to drive all that way, because according to him, he'd "seen all those pageant-type things before." But experiencing the show was another turning point for him. He loved it! The cast members, from "Jesus" to "Peter," took him in and basically loved him into the Kingdom. For years, my dad was the ambassador in West Texas for *The Promise*.

Later, when my eighty-two-year-old dad fell and injured himself (necessitating surgery) and was confined to the hospital for about a month, one of his nurses challenged him with, "Mr. Norman, as nice a man as you are, you don't need to be a'cussin'."

"Well, I can't help it."

"Sure you can! I'll help you. Every time you say a bad word, I'm gonna put a mark up here on this poster board."

Three weeks later, a new mark hardly ever appeared on that board.

Dad moved into an assisted-living facility after his release from the hospital, and the preacher who gave short sermons there on Sunday afternoons personally invited him to attend. He went once and never missed again. Over the next three years my dad became gentler, more accepting, more forgiving, more sensitive to others' feeling, and less sensitive to things that didn't matter. He gave up alcohol, too. Yep, he was a changed man. The good Lord has a way of doing that to a person.

One day back in 1965, my high school health teacher asked for those whose fathers had taught them about "sex" to raise their hands. In a class of thirty, I was the *only* one who raised a hand. It made me think. I was (am still) proud to be named Charles III after my daddy, Charles Henry Norman Jr.

23

A PRESENT-DAY FISHER OF MEN

Twenty-three years ago, my father was finally persuaded to come see the Christian musical drama *The Promise* at the Texas Amphitheater in Glen Rose. It was like pulling teeth to get him there. Even though his two grandchildren had roles in the show, he was reluctant (may I say stubborn?) to attend. He said, "I've seen all those pageant-type things before." In reality, I believe it was because he didn't want to be confronted with anything "religious." Nevertheless, in September of 1996, my dad relented and attended *The Promise*. It was a life changer for him. He could not get over seeing his grandchildren, Charles and Noelle, on stage in such a grand production. He'd never seen such a "pageant" in all of his seventy-four years. From start to finish, he was fully engaged in the songs, the characters, and the message.

But of all the actors in the show, there was one man who really got to my dad. The character was the Apostle Peter, and he was played by a local resident named Allen. The thing was, "Peter" was rough around edges, unkempt, boisterous, and impulsive to a fault, which was just the antithesis of the type of guy I figured my dad would be drawn to. Yet, after the show, there was Allen with his long, scruffy hair and beard. He was standing there talking to my dad. They were up on the grass landing of the amphitheater, where cast members and audience members mingled and

greeted one another. It was strange seeing my strait-laced dad befriending such a character. I'd never seen that before.

My widowed father became a regular at *The Promise* for the next several years and was Allen's biggest fan. Whenever Allen was about to sing or act out his scene in "Peter's Song," my dad would lean over to me and whisper, "Here he comes. I love this part." It was the passion, emotion, sincerity, and believability in his rendition of the song that touched my dad. Though he could not identify with Peter's rugged, shabby appearance, he identified with Peter's deep inner struggles and numerous faults, along with his desire to do right while still doing wrong and his desire to cry out to the Lord for help and forgiveness. Maybe that's something that we can all identify with.

Over time, my dad and Allen became more than friends; they became brothers in Christ, so much so that my father made it known that when the time came, he wanted Allen to sing at his memorial service. That time did come around ten years later, and Allen played piano and sang Kris Kristofferson's song "Why Me Lord?" The lyrics clearly represented my believing father's last years on Earth.

Fast-forward to present day. I've recently learned that Allen, who lives in East Texas, is battling stage-four prostate cancer. The prognosis is not good. We've talked on the phone, and I told him more of what he meant to my dad. He knew some of the story, but not all of it. I told Allen that out of *all* the characters in *The Promise*, I would've thought he would be the most unlikely to connect with my father. Yet what did I know? God's ways are not our ways. His are better. Perfect, in fact. As our conversation was winding down, we cried a bit as we reminisced about how the Good Lord providentially brought them together, and we reflected on the eternal good that came from their friendship.

I'll always be grateful for Allen, especially for how he used his gifts and talents to reach out to my dad (and I'm sure countless others), who needed to hear the Good News. Just as the true Peter was to become a "fisher of men" at the behest of the Savior, Allen was a fisher of men for my dad. Because of Allen's faithfulness (and others' faithfulness, too) to the Great Commission, my dad is in heaven, and he's awaiting the sweet reunion he'll have with Allen and other true believers. One day, Allen will most assuredly hear the Master say, "Well done, my good and faithful servant."

Thank you, Allen, my dear brother, for your obedience to the Great Commission and for the enduring influence you had on my family. Amen.

Addendum: Allen Conley entered the gates of heaven a couple of weeks after the article was first published. He did read this piece. He told me that he had been very blessed and that he was honored to have known my dad and to have been used by the Lord in my dad's life.

Unlikely friends who became brothers.

24

RETURN DOG TO SENDER

Years ago, back in 1980, I was living in Nashville and was the proud owner of a year-old Cockapoo named Shadrach. Because of a job relocation, I could no longer care for Shad. Parents to the rescue! My folks agreed to take Shad off my hands and have him as their dog. So, I shipped ol' Shad from Tennessee to Odessa. I was sad, relieved, and grateful all at the same time. My folks answered the call. That's just what parents do.

Fast-forward to 2008, when my own son asked us to take in Kalli, his "roommate" and year-old hyper, untrained beagle. He'd gotten the dog because he wanted a companion and, I think, because it was a possible conversation starter with the ladies. But with Kalli not being completely house broken, I'd say there were definite limitations. When Charles graduated from college, he, too, was in transition and needed someone to take Kalli, at least temporarily. Carolyn and I agreed to take the dog until our son got settled into his new job and apartment. What goes around comes back around, and my dog situation was coming back to bite me.

Well, we'd had her at our house out in the country for a couple of weeks, and then one day Kalli just disappeared. We made a modest effort to try and find her. We searched the area and called around to neighbors, local vets, and Animal Control, but we had no success. Now, I love animals, especially dogs, but I have to admit that we were not too upset. Surprisingly, neither was Charles. He seemed quite okay with her disappearance, actually. Was she cramping his freedom and lifestyle a little bit?

About two weeks later, I got a call from an older fellow up in Ft. Worth, and he asked if I was missing a beagle. I thought, *Oh no, here we go again.* He'd tracked me down from the tag on her collar and definitely wanted me to come get her. Apparently, she had been picked up somewhere near our property, had been driven up to Ft. Worth, had gotten loose (or had been let loose?), and had run right to this guy's house. I did feel obligated to take her back, so I agreed to meet him the next day, as I was on my way home from the DFW Airport after being on a trip out of town. We rendezvoused in a Walgreen's parking lot at the appointed time. I gave him some money for his trouble and thanked him for contacting us. He seemed as relieved to let her go as I was distressed about taking her back. Whatever.

I put Kalli in the backseat, her leash loosely tied to the passenger headrest, and then I was homeward bound. I'd been clipping along I-35 South for a few minutes when, all of a sudden, I started smelling this putrid, horrible odor that was emanating from right behind me. I was thinking, *What is that?!* I glanced behind me, and that dog had pooped all over the seat and was hopping all around. She even put her filthy front paws on the headrests of the front seat! To make it worse, the dog seemed happy as a lark. She was just jumping all around, almost as if to say, "Hooray! I'm headed home! I'm headed home!" I lowered my window, and in a complete role reversal, I was sticking *my* head out the window for fresh air. I had forty minutes to go.

Thank the good Lord for cell phones. I got ahold of Carolyn and told her about my worsening predicament. When she finally stopped laughing (which only aggravated me more), we came up with a plan. She met me in the driveway, and she was all decked out in what looked like one of those "hazmat" suits, complete with a face mask, goggles, overalls, gloves, and a cap. She had paper towels, disinfectant spray, a scrub brush, and a water hose at the ready. You name it, she had it. I was hoping she'd start with me, but oh no, she had the "Let's welcome Charles's prodigal dog back home first" attitude. Ha! I scurried off to the shower, and within the hour I was clean, the car had been cleaned, and Kalli was bathed and content. Now, I always looked forward to coming home and seeing the pretty wife after out-of-town trips, but this took the cake. I don't think she's ever looked as good to me as she did that day, hazmat suit and all.

25
SEPTEMBER 11, 2001 — WHY NOT ME?

I am writing this on the eighteenth anniversary of the 9/11 terrorist attacks that happened in our country. Each year's remembrance takes me back to a time in my life when I felt especially grateful, humble, blessed, and a little unworthy. You see, I had been working as a flight attendant with American Airlines that infamous morning. My plane from Tampa, FL, had just landed at DFW, and upon arrival at the gate, we got the word. We heard the announcement saying that all flights across the US were henceforth cancelled until further notice, and all passengers, crews, and airport personnel were to vacate the terminals. It was a surreal feeling being among the hordes of people, hardly talking, just shuffling our way out through the exits. Though we didn't really know exactly how our world was going to change, all of us knew things were going to be different. At the time, we couldn't envision all of the ramifications that would result from the horrific events that were unfolding in real time some 1,300 miles to the northeast of Dallas/Fort Worth Airport.

As the hours and days passed and we began to learn more about the actual events, my interest turned to the seventeen AA crew members who perished in the two American Airlines planes that had crashed that day. Having worked with American for a number of years, and having been based in Chicago, Washington DC, Nashville, and Dallas/Fort Worth, I knew there was a possibility that I had flown with one or more of the crew members somewhere along the line. As more information became public and the names of the crew members were released, I was somewhat selfishly relieved that I did not personally know any of the crew members who died that day.

However, there *was* one person in particular who caught my attention. He was the captain of AA flight #77, which was the plane that had originated from Dulles Airport (VA) and that had been flown into the Pentagon. His name was Charles Burlingame III. It just so happens that I am also a Charles III. Then I read that Captain Burlingame was fifty-one years old. He was a college graduate, was married, and had a daughter. I was starting to think, *Hmm, I'm fifty-one years old. I'm a college graduate, I'm married, and I have a daughter.* Charles had lived in a Virginia suburb west of Washington, DC, had been with American for fifteen years or so, and had been based out of Washington, DC. Me, too! I found out that one of his parents (his dad) was born in 1923 and had died a few years before 9/11. My mom was born in 1923, and she, too, died seven years prior. Captain Burlingame had served in the US Air Force and had the nickname "Chic." My dad had served in the Army Air Corps (later to become the US Air Force) and had gone by the name "Chick" during those years. Furthermore, early that fateful morning of September 11, 2001, Captain Charles Burlingame and I both took off in our American Airlines jets, leaving eastern US cities and heading west toward our destinations, which were both hours away. I made it. He didn't.

After considering all of the similarities Captain Burlingame and I had at that moment in time, I couldn't help but think, *My goodness, that could have been me!* As I tried to assimilate these things that Captain Burlingame and I shared, I couldn't help but feel especially fortunate to still be around. For solace and better understanding, I turned to my Heavenly

Father, my Creator. Scripture verses that I knew came to mind and heart. In Psalm 139, I am told that before I was even born, the good Lord had scheduled each and every day of my life and recorded them in His Book. In the book of Job, He tells us that He, and He only, is the giver and taker of life. In Psalm 31, we're reminded that "Our times are in His hands." I thought of Captain Burlingame's family and the thousands of other families who were having to cope with such a tragic personal loss. I hurt for and with them. Only through God's grace could one begin to find comfort in such a time of deep sorrow and grief. I pledged to be mindful and grateful for each day I have on this Earth, counting every day as a gift from the one who made me. Amen!

26

ROOTING FOR THE UNDERDOG

With football season right around the corner, I can hardly wait to cheer on my teams: the Odessa Bronchos, the Glen Rose Tigers, the Texas Tech Red Raiders, and the Aggies of Texas A&M. And oh, this year I've added one more: Ft. Worth's Diamond Hill-Jarvis Eagles. You see, the DHJ varsity football team is in the midst of the nation's *longest* losing streak. Seventy-seven consecutive losses. Three more defeats in a row, and they will tie the all-time *national* record for consecutive losses in the history of high school football. Without a doubt, this is a record the team wants to avoid, along with the stigma that would naturally follow.

As the Eagles prepare for their season opener on August 30, I'd like to share my thoughts about and perspective on their situation. This is coming from someone who not only loves the game of football but who also loves young people. So, this is an open letter to the DHJ team:

> *Win or lose tonight, you are still winners! To go out there, even with the circumstances that surround you, and play for your school and represent your classmates on that field...well, that says something about you from the get-go. Your value in life is not determined by whether you win or lose this first game of the year, or the next game, or all of the games this year or the next. You all deserve credit for just getting on the field and doing the very best you can. That's all your coaches, teammates, family, friends, and fans can ask.*
>
> *As you get older and these high school days fade into memory, the way you look at things in life will change. As important as it may seem to you now (and it is important), these football games will become less and less significant in the grand scheme of things. Five years from now (or ten or twenty), most likely only a handful of people will know you played football for Diamond Hill. Your true worth as a person is not determined by athletic feats of grandeur (or lack thereof). The people around you will be more concerned about who you are as a person and what kind of character you possess. Are you honest, dependable, loyal, unselfish? Are you a hard worker and a team player for your company and fellow workers? Do you go the extra mile and persevere when times get tough? You can develop these quality traits right there on the football field, and this will help you prepare for the bigger battles of life that are coming your way.*
>
> *Have fun and enjoy this time. Not everyone has the chance, or the talent, to play varsity football. You do! Respect your coaches. Love on your teammates. The bonds you form with these guys will last a lifetime. Remem-*

ber, you are all in this together. Savor these moments. Whether you end the day in victory or defeat, this time, too, shall pass. And one day, you can stand tall and say, "I was there, and I did my best."

Finally, thank the good Lord in heaven, the one who made you, for giving you the opportunity and ability to play football for your school. The Good Book exhorts us all to acknowledge our Creator and put our trust in Him. If you do this, you will "soar on wings like eagles, and you will run and not grow weary."

Come Thursday night, August 30, there will be an extra contingent of fans in the stands at Ft. Worth's Scarborough-Handley Field. They will be standing with and cheering for the DHJ Scarlet and Black as they take on the visitors from Dallas Conrad. Though these fans really "have no dog in the fight," so to speak, they will be pulling for the underdogs at Diamond Hill-Jarvis. As Americans, we just naturally like to do that.

Addendum: Diamond Hill-Jarvis won the game 40–12, thus ending the nation's longest losing streak and keeping the team from tying the all-time record. A contingent of fourteen fans from Cleburne/Glen Rose attended the game and cheered the Eagles to victory.

27
YOU'VE GOT A FRIEND IN ME

On Valentine's Day this year, my oldest grandson, eight-year-old Chaz, went with a few other classmates from his elementary school to visit a nursing home in a neighboring community. This group of a dozen or so second graders ventured up there to hand out Valentine's Day cards and to bring some cheer to a few of the residents living there.

They split up, and Carolyn accompanied a group of about five boys as they made their way down one wing of the facility. At the end of the hall, they entered Chuck's room, where they encountered a fifty-five-year-old black man who was dozing off in his wheelchair. But Chuck was ready to talk to anyone who cared to visit. The boys gathered around him, gave him a card, shared a few words, and then hugged him as they left. Carolyn told me that Chuck was so overcome with emotion that he began to weep, just because someone took the time to come in, say hello, and wish him a good day.

When Carolyn told me about this, I couldn't help but feel compassion for this man, and in turn, I felt compelled to go meet this lonely soul. So, it was a few days later when I made the hour-long drive to see Chuck. He perked up when I entered his room and introduced myself. We connected fairly quickly, and I found out a few things. Chuck's real name was Charles, like mine. He had diabetes and had no family to visit him (they'd all moved out of state). He did get out of the nursing home three times a week for a few hours, as he went for kidney dialysis every Tuesday, Thursday, and Saturday. That was it. He said the food was pretty good at the nursing home, but he told me that he sure missed the good eatin' at his favorite local place, Golden Corral. Apparently, it had been years since he'd been there. He told me that the staff in the nursing home was nice and friendly but that he had no real friends who came and saw him.

It was then that I said, "I will be your friend, Chuck. You've got a friend in me now."

"Really?"

"Yeah."

"Thank you," he said as tears filled his eyes.

Tears filled mine, too. I asked Chuck if he had ever played sports.

"Yeah, football was my favorite. I was the running back in high school. Scored some touchdowns, too."

"Oh, that's great, Chuck. Not me. I wanted to, but I was too scrawny."

He chuckled a bit, and it was a light moment for a man who could no longer walk.

Chuck did have kids (ten of them, actually, and with three different women), but they were all in different places and had chosen not to have any real relationship with him. I sensed that he had deep regret for the way things were, and he started crying as he told me about his youngest, his twenty-something "baby girl."

As we continued our conversation, I was just drawn to this gentle, remorseful, soft-spoken, sensitive man of color. I felt so sad for him. After asking God to help me speak, these words just came: "Chuck, I want to tell you something I've never told anyone before. You see, I grew up out in West Texas in the fifties and sixties, and I never knew any black folks.

So much of our society was segregated, and the blacks and whites pretty much stayed to themselves. As I got older, I went off to school and traveled quite a bit, and I became aware of some things. Disturbing things. Racial prejudices and injustices. Things I never understood or experienced while growing up. Later, Chuck, after becoming a real Christian, it made me want to reach out and befriend people like you." The words just seemed to flow out of my mouth. "I bet you've had times in your life when you've been mistreated, cursed at, called names, discriminated against, threatened, or even bullied by white folks simply because of the color of your skin. Is that right, Chuck?"

He nodded as he looked down, wiping away the tears.

I continued. "Chuck, I am here to apologize for them — all of them — from the bottom of my heart. I am so sorry those things happened to you. They should have known better. They were wrong, and they were ignorant. You know what, Chuck? No matter what, regardless of what you have or haven't done, I consider you equal to me in *all* things. You know why, Chuck? Because our God in heaven created you *and* me in His image!"

Chuck once again starting crying, and through his tears he said, "Thank you for saying that. That means a lot to me."

And finally, I said, "Do you believe in God?"

"I love God."

"Chuck, do you believe in Jesus?"

"Oh, I love Jesus."

"Me, too. And you know what that means, Chuck? It means that not only am I gonna be your friend, but I'm gonna be your *brother*. Your blue-eyed soul brother!"

A few days later, I got a takeout meal for him from Golden Corral. Oh, how he loved that!

"What'd you like best, Chuck?"

"That piece of fried catfish! It was so good. But I'm really not supposed to have it."

"Uh, oh...sorry 'bout that. I won't tell if you won't."

We both smiled slyly and agreed to keep it in the family.

Addendum: In November 2020, Chuck exchanged the confines of a lonely room in a Texas nursing home for the place the Lord Jesus prepared for him in Paradise. No more tears or suffering far this gentle soul, for he now sings with angels and 10,000 years from now will still be doing the same.

28

BIRD REHAB BRINGS RICH REWARDS

My wife, Carolyn, loves all animals, but she has a special affinity for birds. She's always puttering around the house; putting up new feeders, birdhouses, or baths; and luring any and all birds with her combination of seeds, fruits, suet, and insects. She gets pictures of any new species that might be flying in to nest and any species that might just be passing through Carolyn's Bird Haven. On the calendar, each year, she documents the first day of arrival for the various migrating birds (hummingbirds, especially), and she is particularly pleased when a new species chooses to try out her newest bird B&B. No payment is required, though it seems the birds never fail to leave an obligatory deposit. I guess "the chirp" is out that the Normans have quite an avian buffet ready for all newcomers and regulars.

About ten years ago, Carolyn agreed to take in and nurture three crow fledglings. What an adventure that was! I was not too keen on this endeavor. Let me explain. The first day we had them, unbeknownst to me, Carolyn had placed them in a large box on top of the washer in the laundry room. I walked in on those birds, and they let out an ear-piercing "Caw, Caw, Caw!" Well, I let out a little something myself, and I'll guarantee you it wasn't a "Caw." (Glad the preacher wasn't around. 'Bout scared me to death!)

Regardless, she adopted these feathered friends and named them Dewey, Edgar, and Fiddler. They began to trust and recognize her. She'd feed them several times a day, and soon they could perch and hop around pretty well. The best I could do was "tolerate" these noisy, demanding creatures, but then the day came when Carolyn designated me the official "birdsitter of the day" while she went off to work. It was my duty to tend to these pests, or...um...young birds. Uninspired, but with food in hand, I went around the corner of the house and went to the side yard, where the crows were all positioned on their perch. They saw that I had their bird breakfast in the bucket, and when I hollered, "Okay, birds, I got food," lo and behold, those birds jumped off their perch and came hopping at me like three ravenous puppies. Frightened me a little bit, actually. As my daddy would say, "Dangdest thing I ever saw." Well, I hated to admit it, but that was a turning point for me, and I conceded to the adoption.

Over the next couple of weeks, those birds got to the flying stage and sort of became pets along the way. They were smart and could identify us immediately. Shoot, we could walk outside, clap our hands, and holler for them, and here they'd come, swooping in from trees from afar. They'd land on our shoulder or outstretched arms, or in Carolyn's case, her head (Edgar had a thing for blondes). As much as we enjoyed this endeavor and the mutual relationships that we developed with these birds, we knew it would be best if they didn't become dependent on us. Besides that, they actually did start devolving from "pets" to pests, scratching up the roofs of our cars with their talons, waking us up at the crack of dawn by squawking for their breakfast at the back door, and reminding us of their presence by leaving little "presents" on our patio and porch. Though it took a couple of days of scheming, we were able to lure the birds into cages and take them a few miles away, where we knew there were other nesting crows and plenty of water. Sentimental as it was, letting them go was a good thing to do. The right thing.

More recently, Carolyn had the opportunity to nurture an injured cedar waxwing back to health. She used an eyedropper to give it water and tweezers to feed it a mixture of mealworms, diced blueberries, and grass. Disgusting stuff, really. But not to "CW." He had a voracious appetite and would eat out of her hand. Through Carolyn's flair for care and tender touch, this bird was able to fly within two weeks. We took CW over to a friend's house, where there were other cedar waxwings, and as Carolyn let him go, the bittersweet moment gave way to exhilaration as CW joined his family in the trees. In a deeper sense, there was great satisfaction in knowing that Carolyn had given life and freedom back to one of God's little creatures. For, if the Good Lord knows when a sparrow falls from the sky, then surely He knows when a cedar waxwing takes flight. It warmed our hearts to be part of the plan.

29
RESPECT FOR A MAN OF HONOR

A few years ago, I did some volunteer work for the airline I used to work for out at DFW Airport. On one particular day, while walking through Terminal C, I noticed an elderly gentleman slowly making his way through the crowds of passengers. Figuring this man might welcome some assistance with his carry-on, I approached him and offered to help. That was how I met Mr. Hewitt Gomez. In his mid- to late eighties at the time, Hewitt was on his way from Lafayette, LA, to Albuquerque to attend a gathering of surviving members of an elite group of WWII veterans.

Hewitt told me that he was a veteran of the Army Air Corps and had been part of very select group of secret agents whose mission had been to fly in spies, supplies, and munitions that could aid the resistance against Nazi Germany in Western Europe from 1944-45. Under the code name CARPETBAGGERS, these men flew their purposely black-painted, reconfigured B-24 aircrafts just above the treetops, under the cover of darkness, to minimize detection and maximize their chances of having a safe return to RAF Harrington Base, which was around ninety miles north of London. My new acquaintance shared with me that he had served as a navigator on these nighttime sorties, and he told me that he and his fellow airmen were sworn to secrecy for decades to come.

"Gosh, Hewitt, it must have been quite a frightening experience to go on those clandestine missions."

He replied, "Well, at eighteen years old, I was probably too young to be scared. I just had a job to do."

I escorted Hewitt to his next gate, and he still had time to spare. Being somewhat of a WWII history buff myself, I felt an immediate connection with him and was able to ask him pertinent questions. I sensed that he appreciated that I knew things. I thanked him for what he and his fellow soldiers did to win the war and preserve the freedoms and liberties we have as Americans.

Hewitt had grown up in Louisiana and had been a runner-up national champion in his category of weight lifting (measuring a whopping five feet three; he had been 123 pounds and had been nicknamed "Little Giant"). He still loved college football (LSU) and had actually been one of the first male cheerleaders LSU had ever had (back in 1941). Hewitt was soft-spoken and sharp, and yet all the while he was humble. A man of faith, it was obvious that Hewitt's love of God, country, and family was paramount in his storied life.

What an intriguing fifteen minutes I had with this true American hero! Knowing there would be no food on the two-hour flight to Albuquerque, I offered to buy Hewitt a sandwich and chips so he could take them on the plane, and he took me up on it. Though he offered to reimburse me, I told him, "My goodness, Hewitt, after all you and your generation did for me and mine, this is the least I can do." I knew I had done right.

When we shook hands as a goodbye, we were both at a little loss for words. Providence had brought us together that day. We agreed to stay in touch via phone and email, and we did. Within the year, I made a special trek to Lafayette to have lunch with my friend, and, Lord willing, I was planning to make the hour-long drive to Baton Rouge and LSU afterward. I had always wanted to see the campus and somehow get inside the historic Tiger

Stadium (otherwise known as "Death Valley"). Hewitt was up for it all, and we rendezvoused near the Lafayette Airport at the appointed time. I was in my rental car, and he was in his own vehicle.

I was planning on treating Hewitt to lunch at the place of his choosing, but he indicated that I should just follow him. The next thing I knew, we were pulling up to the Petroleum Club there in Lafayette. His treat. Not only had Hewitt previously worked there as a manager for years, but he was also a hometown hero/celebrity of sorts and had been for decades. Before long, he was introducing me to all of the friends who came over to our table to greet us. I felt a little like Barney Fife at the Esquire Club, for all you *The Andy Griffith Show* fans. It was *me* who felt like the guest of honor.

Over lunch, our like-mindedness became even clearer. We talked about everything from the LSU-Texas A&M football rivalry to racial issues of the past and present. We talked about prostate cancer treatments (both of us were survivors and were receiving the same treatment), and both agreed that we felt blessed to call ourselves Americans.

Then it was on to Baton Rouge and LSU. Hewitt gave me a mini tour of his alma mater, and we got a few close-up pictures of Mike the Tiger (the school mascot, who has his own habitat near the center of campus). Unfortunately, the stadium gates were all locked up. Not to be deterred, we sought out the stadium offices in a building across the street. We took the elevator up and told the receptionist about our strong desire to get inside and view Tiger Stadium for just a few minutes. She seemed a little hesitant, but then Hewitt stepped up. He told her about being an alumnus from the 1940s, about being a former cheerleader, and about being longtime season ticket holder. She seemed to soften up a bit and told us to have a seat while she made a phone call. Within five minutes, Hewitt and I had a private escort who opened up "Death Valley" just for us! What's the saying? It's who you know? What a great day!

A couple of years later, Mr. Hewitt Gomez was honored for his service to our country in front of a 100,000 fans during a mid-field ceremony at the

LSU-Alabama football game. Then, in 2018, Hewitt was awarded the prestigious Congressional Medal of Honor in Washington, DC.

In our conversations over the years, I've almost always told Hewitt that he and the sacrifices of "The Greatest Generation" will *not* be forgotten by my generation. And I've told him that I will remind my two grown children of how he and his fellow countrymen unselfishly gave so much of themselves so we could all have freedom. And finally, I've told him that I will teach my grandchildren to treasure the legacy that was left for them by the Hewitt Gomez's of the world, and I will encourage them to always cherish, love, and appreciate those who gave so they could have.

Though Hewitt is ninety-five years young and small in stature, he stands as tall as a giant in the eyes of those who personally know him. His and his fellow veterans' courageous acts of heroism and sacrifice only underscore the privilege it is to live in this great land, the home of the brave. I am honored to call this man of honor, Hewitt Gomez, my friend.

Honored to know a "Man of Honor."

30

BE CAREFUL WHAT YOU WISH FOR

You know how it was in high school. There always seemed to be a teacher you wanted to avoid if at all possible. That was the way it was for me (and a lot of others) right before my junior year at Odessa High. "Stay clear of Miss Manitzas!" everyone said. They all said she was tough and very strict, and she went by the book, ran a tight ship, and gave lots of homework. So, when I found out that I was going to have Miss Boyd, a new teacher who'd just moved to Odessa, I was elated. Whew! Well, my elation was very short-lived. Miss Boyd was an older version of Miss Manitzas, and what you got with her were dourness, authoritarianism, and extreme pickiness. What a downer!

She was especially particular about grammar, punctuation, and diction, and rarely, if ever, did she give A's. I once got docked ten points for using the ampersand ("&") in an essay, and the thing was, I had learned that handy little abbreviation from my mother, who was a substitute schoolteacher. When I questioned Miss Boyd about why she docked points, she said that in class on Monday she had discussed avoiding such abbreviations in schoolwork. I told her that I had an excused absence and had not been in class on Monday. She said, "Either way, Mr. Norman, it's your responsibility to find out the lessons you missed. You still get a C." I was not a happy writer.

I asked my friend and classmate Jesse if he'd ever gotten an A in Miss Boyd's class. "Not yet," he said. If Jesse didn't get an A, something was wrong. Our future class valedictorian and a future honors graduate from Rice University, Jesse was the only genius I'd ever known personally. For example, the school district required that all students in freshman through senior English classes memorize a minimum of one hundred lines of poetry and recite them in class. This would usually be done over the course of a semester, reciting several short- to medium-length poems. But oh no, not Jesse. Two years earlier, as a ninth grader, he had recited the *entire* eighteen stanzas of Edgar Allan Poe's "The Raven" in one "standing." Not me. I fulfilled my dreaded English requirement by reciting several short poems of insignificance every few weeks. I promptly (and may I say "proudly") forgot the poems the day I said them. I "ain't" no dummy.

I asked Miss Boyd why none of us ever got A's. She replied something like, "Mr. Norman, when you, or anyone else in class, write something comparable to Robert Frost or Emily Dickinson, you'll get your A." I thought, *My goodness, Miss Boyd, we're only sixteen-year-olds. What gives?* Not her.

One day, she gave the class an assignment. "Write out a two to three pages dialogue about an incident or event that happened at school, home, or wherever. No less than three hundred words. It's due on Friday."

I was thinking, *I don't want to do this. I have no idea what to write.* Then...then...the thought came to me: Why not write out a dialogue about what it was like to try to have a conversation with Miss Boyd about grades? You know, about how nobody got an A in her class? I figured I could change the names up a bit. She would be "Miss Bod." I was "Carl." And Jesse became "Jessica." As I was writing it out, I was thinking, *Am I really doing this?* Two and a half pages later, I had it. I read my dialogue over and over. It definitely represented the way my conversations with Miss Boyd went, at least from my end. I told no one (including my parents) about my idea for the assignment. I turned it in on Friday, as scheduled. You know "buyer's remorse?" Well, I had "writer's remorse" almost immediately, and for the whole weekend. What had I done? I didn't feel so well.

So, on Monday, boy, did I dread going to English class?! FDR once famously said, "We have nothing to fear but fear itself." Well, that was exactly what I had: fear itself! When class commenced, Miss Boyd slowly walked around the room, handing out the graded papers, putting each paper facedown on each student's desk. Of course *I* was last. I just knew she was doing this to make me squirm in my seat that much longer. She paused an extra-long amount of time at my desk — for suspense, I guess — and then she placed the paper facedown. I glanced up at her, as she was still hovering over me, and I saw an expression I'd never seen from her before. I didn't know if it was a smirk or a quirky smile. I was thinking, *This is not good.* So I turned my paper over, and what did I see? A-. An A-! She had written on top of the paper, in red ink, *Sometimes it helps to see yourself as others see you. Keep up the good work, Charlie.* As she walked away, she said to me, "I admire the courage it took to write you did." I think I wet my pants.

Over the next few weeks, things began to change for the better. Miss Boyd seemed to ease up some, and every once in a while, we students even caught a glimpse of a smile on her face. Jesse got his A's. And I actually pulled off an A- for the semester. It was hard to believe how things had changed. As strange as it seemed, I actually grew to like Miss Boyd (a little, anyway). I realized that she had taught me well. So well, in fact, that a couple of years later, when I was in summer school at Odessa College, I aced my two college English classes, which were taught by none other than former OHS high school teacher and then college professor Miss Manitzas. I liked her, too!

Addendum: Miss Louise Boyd continued to teach at Odessa High for decades to come...preparing her students to better communicate verbally and through written word in the world they'd soon be facing outside high school. She retired in the mid-1990s and lived her remaining days in Odessa and passed away in 1999. Miss Mary Manitzas also continued teaching and in administration with Ector County Independent School District for 36 years retiring in 1994. She's now 85 years young (as of this writing) and resides in the Austin Texas area. She remembered me and loved this story...enough so, she even read it over the phone to her brothers living out of state. She and I have become friends, and insists that I call her "Mary" whenever I call. Who'd ever "thunk" that some 55 years ago? Not me...or is it "I"?

Miss Louise Boyd
Junior English – Odessa High

Miss Mary Manitzas
Sophomore English – Odessa College
(New friend)

31

WWII VET IS STILL THE TEACHER

One of the first movies my dad took me to see was *The Longest Day*, the 1962 award-winning, epic story about the D-Day invasion on the beaches of Normandy, France, on June 6, 1944. Though I was only twelve years old when the movie came out, too young to comprehend it all, it still made an indelible impression on me.

If you know the history, you know that this invasion involved over 156,000 Allied troops (mostly from the US, Great Britain, and Canada), and it proved to be the turning point in the war in Europe. Actually, it turned out to be a turning point in world history itself. Little did I know that around fifty-seven years later, in little ol' Glen Rose, Texas, I would come to know someone who had stormed those perilous beaches with the first wave of Allied soldiers that fateful day. He did so for me and you. This person was George, who, as I mentioned before, was in a nursing home. I went to visit him after seeing his son at my high school reunion. George was ninety-four at this point. He was wheelchair-bound and didn't get out much anymore. But he could talk some, and for those who would listen, this brave soul had tales to tell and wisdom to share.

George was part of a sixteen-man Army Air Corp, anti-aircraft crew that came ashore on Omaha Beach at daybreak that morning. It was like a bloodbath, with over four thousand Allied soldiers giving their lives that day. George told me that he hadn't been scared. He had been too young, too innocent, and too naïve to understand the reality of what he was facing. He told me that they were all just doing the job they signed had up for, and he gave any credit to those who gave the ultimate sacrifice. Besides being part of the crew that shot down four enemy aircrafts that were trying to thwart the Allied invasion that day, one of George's later tasks was to retrieve the bodies of the killed paratroopers that they came across as they made their way inland. Their task was to identify the corpses as best as they could, then place them in body bags so they could be shipped home or prepared for burial. *How did a nineteen-year-old cope with that?*

A recon man and a skilled sniper, George also survived the Battle of the Bulge and eventually marched all the way through Belgium, France, and Luxembourg. He went all the way to Berlin, where the European conflict ended. I asked him if he harbored ill feelings about the German people. He was not bitter, he said, as "it was Hitler and the ruling Nazi Party that were the true enemies." He said he realized that most of the German combatants were men or young boys who were fighting for their country, just as he was. The Nazis gave them orders on what to do, and they had no choice but to fight, or else.

I asked him how the French people felt about the Americans "invading their country" to battle the Germans. He said they were appreciative, thankful, and happy to be free again. "They gave us food and water to help sustain us during our mission," he said.

"How about the German citizens? How did they feel when you entered their country?" I asked.

"They treated us as liberators. Very hospitable. So glad for the war to be winding down and for Hitler to be gone. Some American soldiers even became 'friends' with German families who welcomed us."

When I visited George on the seventy-fifth anniversary of D-Day, I saw a man whose life was winding down, but he still had purpose. He had reminded me that people throughout the world — no matter their race, language, or ethnicity — are still God's creatures, and they all have the basic yearnings for peace, freedom, and love. And we need to forgive and accept people no matter our differences. Before I left George during this visit, I told him that he would not be forgotten and that I would remind my own children and grandchildren of the sacrifices his generation made for us. I asked him if I could hold his hand and say a prayer for him, and he said he'd like that. As I was finishing my prayer of thanksgiving to the good Lord for this good man, George interrupted by saying, "Can I pray, too?"

"Of course."

He grasped my hands even more firmly, and in a weakened, raspy voice, he proceeded to thank God for sending a friend during the winter days of his life and for bringing him cheer on this day. I knew that this was a special moment. I mean, here was this frail, elderly warrior who had seen and endured so much, and *he was praying for and about me.* How does one understand that? Once again, I was reminded why George and those of his era are deservingly called "The Greatest Generation." Because of their sacrifices, we Americans have the privilege to live in the most wonderful country *ever.*

P.S. Recently, while visiting the national D-Day memorial in Bedford, VA, I came across a plaque honoring the soldiers who gave their lives that day. It read: "D-Day's success owes an incredible debt to its participants. That you yourself are free and here today is but a portion of their rich and enduring legacy. Treasure it." Amen.

Addendum: *The day this article came out in our little paper, I took a few copies of it to George and his family. George was alone and was in a semi-conscious state at the time. Not knowing for sure if he was even aware of my presence, I told him I had something to read to him. I grasped his hand and softly read this article to my dying friend. When I finished, I sensed a Holy presence in the room, and assuring me that George had heard the reading and would soon be singing with angels. Within the week, he was doing just that.*

32
HAPPY HE WILL BE

A year ago, Carolyn and I had coffee with a longtime friend of mine from my school days in Odessa (TX). Several years earlier, I had reconnected with this guy from my past, and we'd had a great lunch together. We ended up reminiscing for over three hours. Though his real name was "Howard," he'd gone by the nickname "Happy" since the mid-sixties. The thing was, we all knew Happy had only a few months to live. Three months earlier, he had been diagnosed with an aggressive form of abdominal cancer, and the doctors had strongly suggested that he get his affairs in order rather soon. We needed to see Happy, and see him we did. To be honest, we saw Happy "happy." Really.

He and I go all the way back to Crockett Jr. High, when I was in the ninth grade and Happy was a seventh grader. Then we knew each other throughout out years at Odessa High, as well. Little did I know that this scrawny guy with the big personality really looked up to me as a role model. Both of us were of slight build, yet we were still "wannabe" athletes. I went into journalism, and he chose choir, where he became quite the singer...so much so that on occasion he even sang with the soon-to-be-famous Gatlin Brothers. Happy and I had both been on the student council and had been named "most dependable" by our fellow classmates. But I only knew him casually, so I was unaware that he was watching me from afar and that he desired to be like me.

Fast-forward to fifty years later, and there Carolyn and I were, listening to this sixty-seven-year-old dying man tell his story. And what a story it was! After receiving the dire prognosis from his doctors, the word got out, and the following post is essentially what he put on his Facebook page for his family, friends, and associates:

Listen, people. Do not feel sorry for me. I've had a great life, a wonderful, full life. Though death is coming for me within a few short months, I'm gonna keep on a' living. I have no regrets. I've traveled the world over, and I have a wonderful, loving family. So, let's all enjoy and love each other some more during this time we have been given. I've lived my life as "Happy" for around sixty years, so why would I change that now?

Happy told us in person that yes, he'd done his crying (at night while all alone). But he counted each new day as another day to connect with those he loves and to do something good for others.

Happy admitted to having his faults and a few regrets, but he still maintained his "wicked wit." He would just sporadically come out with little quips that had an edgy twist to them. Sometimes it would produce lighthearted uneasiness within the listener, thereby giving Happy the desired reaction and satisfaction. On a bit of a tamer side, he'd say such things like, "I'm gonna miss me, too." And then he'd follow up with, "Now that I've talked enough about me, I'll just sit back and listen while *you* talk about me."

This sharp, affable entrepreneur became a very, very successful businessman in the DFW area, and he was quite the philanthropist to boot. He loved sharing his great wealth with noble causes, charities, and foundations that were designed to help those less fortunate. He especially liked to give to children in need.

He told us he'd met with his pastors, that he was right with God, and that he knew where he was going. He mentioned that he'd even gone back and made amends with those he might have offended in years past (which actually inspired me to action). He was happy mending fences. Happy seemed liberated, content, and surreally optimistic. I guess that's the way people feel when they know their positive influence in the world will continue on, even long after their passing.

At the time, Happy told us that his biggest and last remaining goal in life was to still be around so that he would be able to attend the Child Care Associates fundraising luncheon in Ft. Worth on October 16, where he was going to serve as honorary chairman. He made it. With a cane in hand, he walked on stage and was saluted and honored by the hundreds in attendance that day. The $1,000,000 goal for the charity was met with flying colors. It was his last public appearance.

Happy once told me, "Charlie, you taught me how to be a man." I knew not of this sentiment, and obviously it was quite the exaggeration. Still, I was flattered and felt honored that he thought so highly of me, especially considering the flawed man that I am. To think I might have taught this kind, generous, highly respected soul something is very humbling. Happy taught me and a lot of others how to live while dying — with dignity, generosity, gratefulness, courage, and faith. During an interview, somebody once asked Happy what his secret was for maintaining this kind of attitude in the waning days of his life. For him, the answer was found in the Old Testament, in Proverbs 16:20: *"Those that trust in the Lord will be happy."* If only any of us could do this as well as he did.

After the luncheon, I approached my feeble friend for the last time. I told him what a great example and witness he had been to me and so many others both in life and in death. And I thanked him for being my friend, closing with these words: "Happy, I'll see you on the other side."

He smiled and leaned over to me, and in a soft, strained whisper, he said, "I'll be waiting."

And I believed him.

ABOUT THE AUTHOR

PHOTO BY NOELLE NORMAN OVERTURF

Charlie Norman has been writing columns since he was the first editor of his high school newspaper in Odessa, Texas, in 1968. Since 2017, he has been a "Guest Community Columnist" for his hometown newspaper, *The Glen Rose Reporter*. His article "Yeah, Yeah, Yeah: Music That Moved Us" was recently published in the national magazine *Good Old Days*. He is a 1972 graduate of Texas Tech University (BBA) and a 1974 graduate of the University of Texas in Austin (MA). Charlie and his wife, Carolyn, have made their home out in the country in Glen Rose, Texas (named America's Dream Town in 2004), and they are proud parents of their son, Charles IV, and their daughter, Noelle. They are the grandparents of five wonderful grandsons and a granddaughter (sure to be wonderfully spoiled) on the way.

www.ingramcontent.com/pod-product-compliance
Lightning Source LLC
Chambersburg PA
CBHW060202050426
42446CB00013B/2958